INTRAMURALS:
A TEACHER'S GUIDE

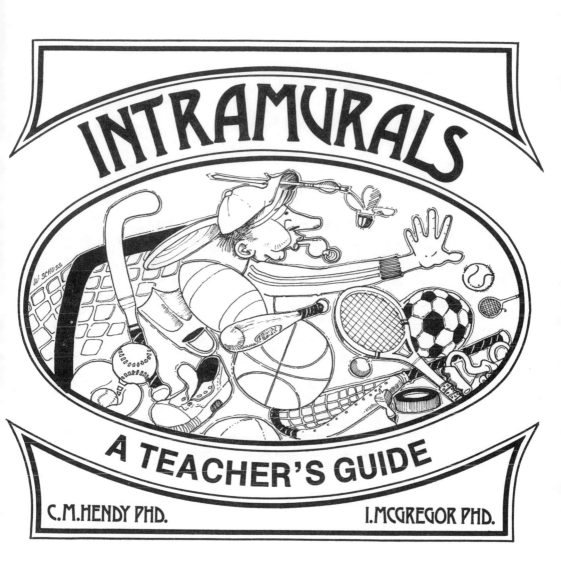

INTRAMURALS

A TEACHER'S GUIDE

C.M.HENDY PHD.   I.MCGREGOR PHD.

Leisure Press
P.O. Box 3
West Point, N.Y. 10996

A publication of Leisure Press.
P.O. Box 3, West Point, N.Y. 10996
Copyright © 1978 by Leisure Press
All rights reserved. Printed in the U.S.A.

ISBN 0-918438-45-4

Photographs by Ed Silva-White and Rodger Lindstrom

Cover design: Bill Schuss

Contents

The vitality, enthusiasm and individuality of a school is reflected, in large part, in its intramural program.

...from the Forward

Foreword

The vitality, enthusiasm and individuality of a school is reflected, in large part, in its intramural program.

The task of arranging and administering intramurals will always fall upon the shoulders of the dedicated and enthusiastic teachers. Since many of these teachers have had no formal background or experience in intramurals, the time consumed in performing this task is generally quite considerable.

Relief and help is definitely in sight for those who are prepared to read this book. The book is unique in that its consciousness makes it a truly useable reference book. Every aspect of the intramural program is adequately dealt with, by listing advantages, disadvantages, and recommendations. The consciousness and quality is bound together in a readable format by the personal observations and recommendations of the authors, both of whom are obviously experts in this area.

I have no hesitation in recommending this book to every elementary and secondary school teacher involved in intramurals.

Alan E. Fischer, President
B.C. Physical Education Society
Abbotsford, April 1977

I welcome the appearance of this much-needed guide to the organization and administration of intramurals in the schools. The book is a comprehensive manual from which teachers at both elementary and secondary levels can select suitable items to organize successful programs.

Michael J. Hardisty, President
B.C. Physical Education Teachers
Association
Coquitlam, April 1977

Intramural credo: An activity for everyone and everyone in an activity.

CHAPTER I
Introduction

This book was not written solely for physical education teachers, in fact, no knowledge of physical education is presumed. The book is designed to be helpful to all teachers regardless of their background and training and of whether they teach at the elementary or secondary level.

Although at various points in the book we have felt it appropriate to make comments specific to the elementary or secondary level, there is really very little difference conceptually in the application of our model to either one. In practice, teachers will quite naturally make allowances for the age of their students, particularly those in leadership roles.

The primary focus of the book is how to start an intramurals program, but these basic considerations will also be useful to someone revamping an existing program. This text is not designed to replace the excellent texts already published on intramurals; rather it is hopeful that the concise, point-form style of this text will provide the reader with a quick and easy guide to the information necessary to develop a quality intramural-recreational sports at any level of schooling.

For any organization, careful planning is vital to accomplish anything worthwhile.

CHAPTER II
Things To Do Before Starting A Progam

For any organization careful planning is vital to accomplish anything worthwhile. Teachers planning intramural programs (hereafter called staff advisors) should consider all students and all staff in the school, plus the appropriate board level administrator and the parents.

The following is a check-list, in chronological order, of things to do before starting a program:

1. Discuss the program and your plans with your P.E. Department Head and other P.E. departmental staff members.
2. Talk to your P.E. Supervisor (if your District has one). Inquire about other intramural programs in your District.
3. Secondary staff advisors should review the intramural programs in their feeder elementary schools.
4. Check resource materials (Appendix 1).
5. Put together a brief presentation to your Principal concerning your plans and goals; include the basic philosophical foundation of your program and your tentative plans for accomplishing your goals.
* 6. Convince your Principal and try to arrange the administration of the intramural-rec sports program as part of your work load.
7. Talk to all coaches at your school.
8. Seek support from all staff colleagues.
9. Seek help from some colleagues; more staff help may be required at the elementary school level.
10. Develop an Intramural-Rec Sports Council.

*11. Fill all positions on Council.
 12. Ask student body what activities they would like to have included in the intramural-rec sports program.
 13. Council plans total program.
 14. Talk to P.E. Department Head, P.E. teachers and all coaches again.
 15. Present program to Principal for final approval.
 16. Inform parents. Out of school time may be involved & some may wish to help.
 17. Start program.

*   The two most important steps are number 6 and number 11. To run an effective intramural program, a teacher needs more than the mere acquiescence of the school Principal. Active support is required and can best be shown by allocating in the staff advisor's work load time for intramural-rec sports administration.

The important requirement in step 11 is to fill the Council positions with capable, enthusiastic and dedicated students. There is no room for passengers on the Intramural-Rec Sports Council. We are not in favour of elections to these positions, preferring instead the recruitment method.

CHAPTER III
Philosophy and Objectives

Philosophy

Sports are not only beneficial for varsity athletes, sports offer something for everyone. That is a basic rationale for intramurals. But the pursuit of excellence is commonplace in the minds of students, and being less than excellent is hard to accept and cope with. From students' early years in school, there is an ever-present pressure to achieve academically — to "pass" into the next elementary school grade, and then later to attain high marks. This outlook carries over into the students' physical activities too, particularly at the secondary level. For most, self-image is very important to students. In the case of many individuals who are not overly physically-talented, they frequently reject organized physical activity. They simply are unwilling to risk putting their ego on the line because of their apparent physical ineptitude.

Few students are taught to cope with this commonplace and quite natural situation. If an activity is worth doing, is it worth doing regardless of the level of performance? Does this mean teachers should encourage mediocrity? Not at all! It means that teachers should encourage students to do their best at all times; but also, and more importantly, teachers should educate students to enjoy physical activity even if the students possess a less-than-excellent level of ability in the skill required for the activity. Quite frankly, most people have only average physical and motor skills — that's what the word average means. Just because someone is a poor basketball player, for example, is no real justification in itself to stop playing the game. Teachers should try to overcome students' self-image problems and emphasize the obvious potential advantages of physical activities. Unfortunately, a lack of skill is a poor motivator to play anything. Since that is a highly complex issue, it should be addressed in formal physical education classes. The most important factor is attitude — to learn and to play — based on self-image. Students should be taught to set appropriate levels of aspiration according to their interests and aptitudes. Not everyone can be a superstar, but everyone can enjoy physical activity and organized sports programs.

Competitiveness is now viewed almost as a dirty word by many teachers, excluding coaches. This is regrettable, since that view is misinformed. Competitiveness is not necessarily correlated with physical skill. Not all interscholastic athletes are highly competitive — to the chagrin of their coaches. By the same token, there are low-skilled students, who can be highly competitive, sometimes to the annoyance of their peers and teachers, but to their own great satisfaction. Intramural sports are for every student and can meet the needs of all, so long as programs are properly structured.

Objectives

Since intramural sports are the recreational application of the physical education program, they have similar objectives. We believe the intramural-rec sports program should promote and provide all students with opportunities for

1. Physical and mental health and fitness.
2. Personal and group enjoyment.
3. Recreation, present and future.
4. Socio-psychological development.

CHAPTER IV

Organization

Intramural-Rec Sports Council
Units of Competition
Classification of Participants

INTRAMURAL-REC SPORTS COUNCIL

The Intramural-Rec Sports Council is the cornerstone of a sound intramural sports program. In many instances, it may profoundly affect the eventual success or failure of your program. Since, in the long term, an effective Council will administer the total intramural-rec sports program with minimum maintenance from you, the staff advisor, we strongly recommend that you choose the Council members yourself. Choose with great care. Frankly speaking, there is no room for non-productive individuals on the Council. In our view, the democratic process of electing Council members is usually just too risky. Of course, even choosing the members yourself gives no performance guarantee, so you should devise performance criteria and a mechanism for replacing under-producers. The honour of being selected to the Intramural-Rec Sports Council will not be treated as lightly if the individual can easily lose the position. (You can even write job descriptions if your program becomes really well-organized).

A proposed organizational structure is presented in Figure 1. The sample Council consists of 6 students (one of whom is elected chairperson) with you acting as the staff advisor. The Council is responsible for administering the intramural sports program in its entirety, and coordinates all committees. The Council is also responsible for formulating and updating an Intramural-Rec Sports Constitution (see sample constitution, Appendix 2). The *1st line* committees of the Council each contain two Council members, with the *2nd line* committees containing at least one Council member. Other members of these 2nd line committees consist of students who have volunteered for positions of responsibility. In elementary schools, a Primary Leaders Committee should be considered as a fourth 1st line committee.

The staff advisor sits on all committees. All 1st line committees, and the Council as a whole, should convene weekly with 2nd line committees meeting when appropriate. Areas of responsibility for each committee are detailed below:

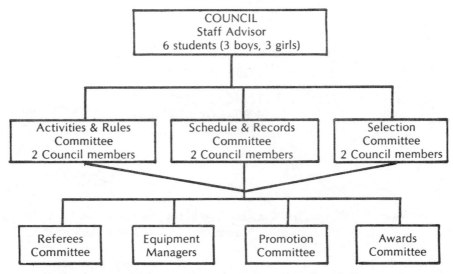

FIGURE 1. A Sample Intramural-Rec Sports Council and Committees

1st Line Committees

Activities and Rules Committee
1. Decides on the activities to be offered during school term. For possible sports, refer to the section on Activities.
2. Sets up rules and regulations to Referees Committee.
3. Establishes and enforces rules on eligibility, participation, protest and sportsmanship (see section on Rules and Regulations).
4. Establishes spectator policy for situations where this may become a problem.

Schedule and Records Committee
1. Draws up all schedules (including times, dates and locations) for all events for the school term (see section on Scheduling).
2. In liaison with the Promotion Committee, keeps the scoreboard up to date with results, standings, scorers, etc.
3. Maintains a suitable system for keeping records.

Selection Committee

1. The main responsibility of this committee is to equalize competition in team events as far as possible on the basis of skill.
2. Since all interested students are placed on teams, the Selection Committee must ensure equal playing time for all participants, regardless of skill.
3. The staff advisor should counsel "stacked" teams and take appropriate action to even things up.
4. Promotion of sportsmanship is a high priority of this committee.
5. In schools with "house systems", the house captains usually function as the Selection Committee.

2nd Line Committees

Referee Committee

1. Assumes responsibility for recruiting and training officials for all events (refer to section on Officiating). This involves running officials clinics for referees, umpires, scorekeepers and linesmen prior to the start of play. Local sporting bodies are often an excellent source of films and/or counselling on officiating.
2. An official's schedule in each activity should be drawn up and posted for the benefit of referees and participants.
3. Any rule change is communicated to team captains.
4. Performance of officials should be monitored. Constructive criticism may be necessary, but this should be handled by the staff advisor.

Equipment Managers

1. Ensure equipment is set up and ready to go prior to the start and returned at the end of each game (report all breakages).
2. One or two managers should be assigned per activity.

Promotion Committee

1. This committee is responsible for publicizing all aspects of the intramurals program from start to finish, from details on sign-up to results (see section on Promotion).
2. It is an important function of this committee to ensure that results are published by the next day at the latest.

Award Committee

The amount of money allocated to intramurals will determine the scope of the awards system at your school. Considerations for this committee are dealt with in the section on Points and Awards.

UNITS OF COMPETITION

The primary consideration in deciding what the units of competition are to be is to achieve a balance between administrative simplicity and high participation. Although various possibilities exist in this regard, no particular system is markedly better than another. Some of the more frequently used methods are summarized below.

Houses

1. This system works well in many schools and is probably the best for the elementary level.
2. The houses are organized according to many criteria, for example:
   a) Alphabetically by surname
   b) Birthdate
   c) Homeroom
   d) Geographical location of home address
   e) Combinations of the above
3. The disadvantages of a house system are firstly that staff leaders are needed for each house and secondly that stacked teams are inevitable. In both cases, participation may be adversely affected.

P.E. Classes

1. Class lists can be used as units.
2. The main advantage of this system is the possibility of correlation between intramural activities and P.E. class activities.
3. Large secondary schools with several P.E. staff members may find this method more useful than other schools.

Draft System

In this system, the Selection Committee (or house captains) would be required to select teams from a registration list. Input into this process would be solicited from P.E. teachers and coaches. The disadvantage is that some students might not want to play for the team to which they are drafted, for a variety of reasons.

Team & Individual Registrations

1. This system is gaining popularity among secondary schools.
2. Its main advantage is that it allows players to form their own teams, enabling students to participate with their friends.
3. Individual registrations (independents) are also encouraged, since *all* players are placed on teams.
4. The Selection Committee plays an important role in ensuring equitable competition, as far as possible. Counselling of stacked teams should, however, be left to the staff advisor, who must take appropriate action

to even out the competition, if this system is to work effectively. This is usually not a major problem as students quickly come to realize the importance of equalization.

Recommendation

We recommend the last system. Although we do not advocate changing from the situation currently employed in your school if it is working reasonably well, we feel that you should give serious consideration to this question.

CLASSIFICATION OF PARTICIPANTS

The main purposes behind the classification of participants are:
1. to equalize competition
2. to reduce the possibility of injury

Classification Systems

1. Grade Level

This covers age groupings but it may not be adequate for activities where height and weight are important. The Selection Committee would be responsible for handling any anomalous situations. Some individual activities (e.g. kite flying, frisbee) are not greatly affected by height, weight and age differences. Combining various grades is therefore possible.

2. Ability, Competitiveness and Sex

The following is a policy statement for the intramural sports program at S.F.U. We believe that such a policy will also work at other schools.

The intramurals program at SFU is structured to meet the needs of a wide spectrum of people. Although competitiveness is not emphasized, neither is it discouraged. Accordingly, we have "A Leagues" for the more competitive and/or more skilled participant, while also offering "B Leagues" in the same activities for the less serious and/or less skilled player. Such a set-up recognizes that there is not always a high, positive correlation between competitiveness and skill level. Thus, for example, a highly competitive, low-skilled participant *might* be encouraged to join A League, whereas a non-competitive but higher skilled player *may prefer* to play B League.

The division into A and B Leagues is the only form of distinction made in the intramurals program. That is to say that with one or two exceptions, we make not separation on the basis of sex. Thus, all intramural activities are advertised as coed, and hence, in floor hockey, for example, women are encouraged to play (recently we had an all

19

women team in the A League). In some sports, for example, volleyball and softball, we insist that each team roster contain a predetermined minimum number of women and maximum number of men. This works extremely well in these and other sports, but would be totally impractical in the more physical sports such as floor hockey, ice hockey, and soccer. Some institutions go further than regulating team rosters. For example, by giving four points for a basket scored by women in coed basketball or by ruling that goals can only be scored by women in floor hockey and soccer, they seek to encourage men to increase women's involvement in games. At SFU we do not make such stipulations since we believe that the results are artificial and that distinctions, as mentioned previously, should be made only on the basis of skill and competitiveness.

Although our program encourages people to participate regardless of their sex, we do recognize that, for various reasons, some women feel uncomfortable playing with men in some activities, and vice versa. Thus, for example, the large difference in skill level between men and women in basketball at SFU necessitates a men's and women's basketball league. Other examples of divided activities are men's and women's soccer tournaments, and women's field hockey.

To reiterate, the SFU intramurals program is predominantly coed. We feel a totally coed program is not practical and accordingly a few of our activities are scheduled for women or men only.

N.B. Ability and competitiveness may be determined by a variety of methods such as

a) a preliminary tournament to rate players/teams prior to the commencement of a league.
b) in some activities, e.g. track and archery, scores can be ranked
c) observation by Selection Committee
d) by asking the players themselves at which level (skill and competitive) they wish to play.

3. Handicapped Students

Give handicapped students the opportunity to participate in the regular intramurals program in events appropriate to them. Clearly, risk of injury is a more important consideration than their chances of success in that event. Where necessary, because of numbers of handicapped students or because of the nature of their handicaps, special programs should be devised. Recognition for this program should be on a par with the regular program, and care should be taken to ensure that it is not regarded as being for the "have nots".

CHAPTER V

Administration

Facilities and Time Allotment
Promotion
Points and Awards
Officiating
Finances
Rules and Regulations
Evaluation
Safety and Legal Liability

FACILITIES AND TIME ALLOTMENT

Often the most difficult problems encountered by teachers trying to run intramural-rec sports programs are lack of facilities or lack of time allotments or both. These problems often seem insurmountable in the face of school bus schedules, half hour lunch periods, school on double shift and so on.

Almost all schools have some form of an interscholastic athletics program. How can these schools arrange for facilities and time for *both* interscholastic and intramural sports programs? While we are in no way trying to get rid of interscholastic athletics (that would be throwing out the baby with the bath water), we strongly believe that intramurals and interscholastic athletics must coexist. Indeed, these programs complement one another. If they are to coexist, however, then school officials must be positive towards the intramural sports program. Each program must be accorded equitable priority. Initially, of course, such a policy may cause problems. However, we believe that such problems can easily be overcome to the benefit of the entire school community especially to the students.

Naturally, if your school doesn't have a particular facility, such as a swimming pool, then you will have to look elsewhere for aquatics facilities. Don't give up, or restrict your intramural sports program to simply the facilities at your school. So long as you can provide proper supervision, non-school facilities quite often can be utilized. See the section on Finances for ideas on facilities.

The Options
1. Before School
Advantages   a) Fewer conflicts with interscholastic athletics program.

Disadvantages   a) Too early a start to the day — may be difficult for students to come early.

                 b) Difficult to persuade staff to come early to work with students, even though many staff arrive early anyway.

                 c) Busing.

2. During School
Advantages   a) There may be enough students free at one time to run a quick special event, e.g. wrist wrestling in a classroom or even a lobby.

                 b) It may be possible to arrange rotating staff supervision of, for example, a table tennis tournament for which students have signed up by time slot.

Disadvantages   a) It depends upon staff willingness to use preparation periods to supervise.

                 b) There is unequal access to events for students.

3. Lunch Time
Advantages   a) All students can be there.

                 b) It is not too early or too late for staff.

Disadvantages   a) If only half an hour is available, this may be too rushed for students and staff.

4. After School
Advantages   a) The students have something to look forward to.

                 b) It is easier to get staff help.

Disadvantages   a) Busing.

                 b) Students with jobs.

                 c) There are conflicts with coaching duties, unless the school also includes intramurals as part of the teaching load.

                 d) If you use interscholastic athletes as officials, they may have a game or practice.

                 e) Teachers may want to be free for preparation, marking, meetings, or they may just wish to get away from students for the day.

5. Evenings and Weekends

Advantages   a) It may be the only time you can use non-school facilities, e.g. Sunday afternoon bowling.

b) Can profitably be used for occasional special events, e.g. aquatics gala, winter carnival, sports night, parents' night.

Disadvantages   a) It may be difficult to obtain school space at night if an outside group has it booked on a regular basis.

b) On weekends it may be difficult to obtain janitorial services required.

Recommendations

1. Use all available times for intramural sports activities.
2. After school is generally best.
3. Wherever possible, avoid scheduling conflicts with big school events (athletics, dramatics, music).

*"But I'm working over 50 hours per week now", you say. If you are really serious about intramural sports, you have to make a choice. You can't do it all.

PROMOTION

This is a difficult but essential aspect of a properly administered intramural sports program. For our purposes, promotion may be viewed very simply as a combination of publicity (before an event) and recognition (after an event). With poor publicity and no recognition, a program may have birth problems and likely soon die. Whereas at the other extreme you may be swamped by more participants than you can handle and overwhelmed by their enthusiasm. The choice is yours.

While administering your program, remember these points:
1. A well-planned, interesting program will attract students
2. Equal participation for all will attract the non-athlete of both sexes
3. Satisfied participants do the best publicity
4. Recognition is a powerful motivator to participate.

Publicity

The Promotion Committee can use three methods to notify participants: written, verbal and photographic.

1. Written

a) Have a notice board(s) solely for intramural sports in a focal point (see section on Recognition).

23

b) Design a logo for intramural sports and use it on all posters, bulletins, circulars or a handbook.

c) Stylish posters are more effective than crude ones and will also impress your colleagues.

d) If your school has no newspaper or you cannot obtain adequate space and/or coverage, consider a separate intramural sports broadsheet.

2. Verbal

a) Use the school public address system if you can, but be brief.

b) Announcements in each homeroom can often be made by students.

c) Any large audience such as school assemblies, sports events and theatricals, make good opportunities for publicity.

d) Physical education classes are excellent vehicles to promote intramural sports, especially if the latter's scheduling has been correlated with the instructional program.

3. Photographic

a) Both stills and home movies or video tapes are good for new student orientation or PTA evenings. Principals tend to favour this kind of activity.

b) The above also makes an excellent project for the school Camera Club.

Recognition

People love to read about, hear about and see photos of themselves and their friends. So pander to your public; trade upon this aspect of human nature.

1. Written

a) Use the intramural sports broadsheet to report results and also to publicize upcoming events. Search out embryonic sports writers

b) Post results promptly and keep league standings up to date

c) Publish school intramural sports records whenever appropriate

2. Verbal

a) Use the P.A. system for noteworthy results, even news flashes, so long as you do it prudently.

b) Reinforce the recognition by casual comments to the student(s) in class.

3. Photographic

a) Take photographs of winning teams and individuals; whenever possible be sure to include the officials.

b) Shoot "this week's participant" chosen at random with the caption "Is this you?" or something similar.

c) Show the "best participant of the month" based on performance and include details of it.

    d) Run mystery photos.

    e) Use a (glass-front) notice board for publicity messages and promotional efforts.

Other Methods
1. Banquet
    a) Run an end of year party/dance.

    b) Give out recent awards then, but introduce *all* prior winners.

    c) For team winners introduce only a representative (there will be great applause from the teammates).

    d) Don't make Fall winners wait until June for their awards; delayed gratification is not a motivator in this case.

    e) Don't forget your officials at the banquet.

2. All star games
Play the games in front of the whole school with all the accompanying frills, e.g. score clock, timekeeper, etc. These games can take the form of:

    a) IM champs vs. student all stars

    b) IM champs vs. teachers

    c) IM champs vs. last year's champs of same grade (includes graduates)

POINTS AND AWARDS

Points Systems
1. There are two kinds of points system—performance points and participation points.
2. For round-robin play, whether league or tournament, you will need to keep records, so at least a simple performance points system will be required, e.g. 3 win; 2 tie; 1 loss; 0 forfeit.
3. Those simple performance points are the only ones you really need to run your intramural sports program, but there are more elaborate points systems which you should at least certainly consider for your school. If you adopt the expanded points system outlined here, your students should have little difficulty doing the clerical work once they have mastered the principles.
4. The main reason for using more elaborate points systems is to promote participation, not only by the typical non-participant (though points alone will not do this) but also by broadening the interests of the typical participant. You have to decide whether, in your school, the end justifies the means.
5. To promote participation, especially when the units of competition are fixed, like Houses, you can emphasize participation points by weighting. In Figure 2, the participation points are much larger than 1st place performance points for both leagues and tournaments.

Team	Ind./Dual	Performance	Team or League	Ind./Dual or Tournament
Basketball	Badminton	1st	45	25
Bowling	Golf	2nd	35.	20
Curling	Kite Flying	3rd	30	16
Floor Hockey	Swimming	4th	25	14
Softball	Table Tennis	5th	20	12
Volleyball	Tennis	6th	15	10
etc.	Track			
	Wrist Wrestling			
	etc.			
		Participation	75	45

FIGURE 2.* Sample Scoring Plan for Team and Individual Activities.

*Adapted from Michigan State University plan: see p. 6., reference #1), Appendix 1. (used with permission of the publisher)

> Example: For participating in a league, all teams receive 75 points. This is far greater than the winners' bonus of 45 performance points. The fifth place team would thus receive 95 points (75 + 20). Use large numbers to your advantage, for higher scores usually bring higher satisfaction to the students.

6. The disadvantages of this method are that students may be pushed by their peers into a competition in which they are not really interested or even physically unprepared. As we have mentioned in Chapter 3, there is nothing wrong with students being competitive, but you should monitor this potential peer pressure rather carefully to ensure that the needs of the participants are being properly met.

7. You can award more of both participation points and performance points for team sports, because more players are required, than you award for individua/dual sports.
> Example: A third place finish in basketball would earn 105 pts. (75 + 30), whereas the third place finisher in table tennis would earn 61 pts. (45 + 16). Note the more complicated example in 9 below.

8. Similarly, you can award more of both points for league play, as more separate attendances are usually required, than you do for tournaments.
> Example: The league runner-up in softball earns 110 pts. (75 + 35), while the runner-up in a tennis tournament earns 65 pts. (45 + 20)

9. The system outlined in Figure 2 has the flexibility to handle more complicated situations which may occur in your program.

Examples: a) Basketball is normally considered a team sport and as such the larger scoring scale would be used. But there are situations where the lower scale is more appropriate, for example for a tournament, or for 2-on-2 basketball.

b) Table tennis is considered an individual/dual sport. It is possible, however, to have team table tennis with say five players (1 singles, 2 doubles) and to run a league. In this case, you should use the larger scoring scale.

10. The performance points scale shown in Figure 2 runs to 6th place. You may decide if you have ten or twelve entries, to give performance points to every entrant. You can do this regularly to promote participation even further, and you may wish to reorganize the points scale with this in mind.

Awards

1. Make sure that your students understand the difference between awards and rewards. Their motivation to play should be intrinsic. Awards should be the means to an end, not an end in themselves. Awards are a by-product of a pleasurable and challenging activity well done, the final stage in a series of satisfactions derived from the activity itself.
2. Keep awards as inexpensive as possible. If your intramural sports budget is large enough to permit the purchase of trophies for teams or individuals, then you may want to consider awards of that nature. Beware however! Don't try to buy participation with "glittering awards".
3. Awards can be made by industrial arts classes and can be either whimsical or serious. The former are often held in higher esteem by students.
4. For team sports, plaques offer several advantages since they have room for many names and are thus long lasting. In many instances, engraving may be done inexpensively at your school. For individuals, certificates are cheap to print and may be run off at school. You may very well have someone at school who is talented at caligraphy. Photographs are good for both teams and individuals, and can be a useful Camera Club project.
5. Awards can be promotional too. For example, team awards can be displayed in a conspicuous location at your school. Another possibility individuals can win T-shirts or patches which automatically advertise the intramurals program.
6. Ensure that individual intramurals awards are quite distinct from your school's interscholastic awards.
7. Consider awards for your officials too.
8. We highly recommend individual and/or team awards for sportsmanship
9. Finally, if your budget will run to it, we recommend a special T-shirt for students on your Intramurals Council. This will be a reward, not award,

for all of their effort. If you have chosen them wisely, you can give them their T-shirts at the beginning of the school year — to advertise the program, to identify them as leaders, and as an act of faith in them for what they are about to do. Wear one yourself too.

OFFICIATING

Rule #1: Referees are always right.
Rule #2: When referees are wrong, see Rule #1.

While good officiating in itself is not THE most important aspect of an intramurals program, poor officiating can ruin any program. It is important, therefore, that referees be selected carefully. You, as the staff advisor, *must* provide substantial guidance in the selection and development of officials. Since *you* know the characteristics in a person that potentially will make them a good official, look for these characteristics in your students. The initial search for officials should be made by the Referees Committee with possible sources as follows:

1. Students enrolled in certain physical education classes can officiate as part of their course requirements.
2. Senior students can be used to referee intermediate games, with the intermediates handling primary level games.
3. We strongly recommend the use of interschool team players for the following (generalized) reasons:
   a) they are interested in their activity
   b) they (should) have greater knowledge of the rules than other students
   c) their judgment in decisions is quite often better than other students
   d) they have the respect of other students
   e) it provides good training for the athletes — they see and appreciate the "other side" of their sport
   f) it may help to bridge the gap between athletics and intramurals
4. Despite our comments in #3, non-athlete volunteers from the general student body may also be excellent officials, so do not ignore this potential source.
5. If your school employs the house system, referees can be attracted by offering points for the house.
6. Some schools employ a "no ref" system in which players call their own fouls. Much initial counselling of participants by the staff advisor is required, but great success is frequently claimed by those employing this system.

Important points which must be taken into consideration by the Referees Committee are as follows:
1. The Referees Committee should meet weekly to discuss rule interpreta-

tion and listen to and advise officials on their complaints. Referees must be given the chance to air their frustrations. Although often very little can be done to accommodate these frustrations, the airing process is usually healthy for all concerned.

2. Officials *must* be recognized, for example, through newsletters, the P.A. system, and photographing the referees with winning teams.
3. Officiating must be for the particular skill level and not to "NHL, NBA, or NFL standards".
4. A teacher should be present at all games.
5. The Referees Committee must stand behind their officials: *never* reverse a decision of an official — only a misinterpretation of a rule.
6. Although the Referees Committee is responsible for the training and on-going evaluation of the officials, any particularly sensitive counselling should be handled by the staff advisor.

FINANCES

The motto here is "a lot for a little". In most instances, an amazingly large number of students can be served at a very low cost. At the secondary level certainly, we believe that the intramurals budget should be separate from physical education and athletics. In these times of shrinking school populations and shrinking educational funding, cost benefit information becomes increasingly important in planning and evaluating school programs. Since school facilities and the equipment provided for physical education classes and athletics may be shared by intramurals, the cost per student for an intramurals program can be very low. As a general rule, then, cost should not be a deterrent to a broad-based program.

Where non-school facilities are utilized in the intramural program, any expenses can be passed on to students either partially or in full. Such programming includes, for example, facilities run by municipal Parks and Recreation Departments (swimming pools, ice rinks, golf and pitch & putt courses), commercial enterprises (bowling lanes, roller rinks, pool halls, crazy golf), or private clubs (curling rinks, golf courses, shooting ranges).

Whenever permitted by local regulations, traditional fund raising methods (for example: car washes, raffles, student labor auctions, etc.) may, of course, be used to raise money for the intramural program. In almost all instances, parent involvement may be helpful. Some schools have even found it possible to accept sponsorship or some form of support from local merchants.

RULES AND REGULATIONS

The Intramural Sports Program Constitution should lay down general guidelines for all aspects of the intramural sports program. The Constitution should be posted on the intramural notice board and all participants (especially team captains) should be encouraged to become familiar with its contents. Special attention should be given to the following points:

Rules
1. Rules should be modified to fit your situation (e.g. gym size, safety, grade or skill level).
2. Major changes in standard game rules should be avoided since it confuses students. If extensive modification is unavoidable, call the game by another name.
3. Rules should include a section on code of conduct and sportsmanship
4. Eligibility rules may vary from activity to activity. For example, inter-school volleyball players may be allowed to play intramural volleyball, but inter-school basketball players may be excluded from intramural basketball (see Regulations 1 & 2 below).
5. Protests should only be made on eligibility questions.
6. Teams should be encouraged to exhibit a high level of sportsmanship at all times.
7. Team captains should be held responsible for ensuring respectful treatment towards the referees by their teammates.

Regulations
   All students are eligible to participate in the intramural sports program. Whenever possible, coeducational activities should be promoted. (see section on Classification of Participants). Interschool athletes should be permitted to compete in the intramural sports under the following conditions:
1. They are not permitted to play in that sport in which they represent the school.
2. An alternate course of action if they are permitted to play in their sport, would be to evenly distribute them among all teams. This distribution can raise the skill levels of all teams. However, the use of outstanding athletes should be strictly controlled to regulate their impact upon the intramural sports program.
3. The number of interscholastic athletes on the floor at one time in any sport should be closely regulated.

EVALUATION

   This important topic has been included under the Administration heading since practitioners often consider evaluation separately. As a result it is all too often overlooked. The two major benefits of continuing evaluation are:
   1) Those aspects of the program which need improvement once identified, can be promptly altered.

2) The effective aspects of the program are identified and emulated in other areas of the program.

Of course, the easy way to discern what is good or bad about your program is to look at the participation statistics: a good quality program should attract large numbers of students. Students themselves are quite subjective about the program and their feelings will determine their involvement. Administrators, including the Intramurals Council, will judge the program largely on statistics. The basic issue is how many students are served and how often.

Objective Evaluation Techniques

There are two methods of producing statistics:
1) manually
2) by computer

1. Manual Statistics

This method involves keeping an alphabetical file card system for each student in your program. Individual or participant statistics are the total number of file cards. Boys and girls can be added separately and the totals can be expressed as a percentage of the student body. For participation statistics, the activities each student undertakes are recorded on each card. Be aware, however, that when you total the participations, you are counting people more than once. To obtain the true total participation involves much more work. You need to count every time a student takes part, e.g. if Jane Doe plays 5 games in a volleyball league, 2 games in a table tennis tournament and enters the kite flying competition, her score is 8. To obtain participations in a league situation, team sheets are required for each game.

Play rate is another statistic which has qualitative as well as quantitative meaning, particularly for leagues. If you schedule 50 floor hockey games and 40 are actually played, you have a play rate of 80%. A high play rate, i.e. a low forfeit rate, indicates satisfaction with the program.

2. Computer Statistics

Secondary schools have turned increasingly to the use of computers for scheduling courses and even for producing report cards. Courses on the use of computers are being taught too. It may well be possible for a school to obtain computer time to produce intramural statistics. At SFU, one of the authors (I.M.), in conjunction with the Computing Center, has developed a computer method of handling intramurals statistics. In addition to producing accurate participant and participation figures, the program also yields 6 other types of output (more than most people need) including a printout of the top intramurals competitor, i.e. the person participating in most activities.

The program is written in Mark IV which requires a large machine. All data to be used is obtained from the registration form, a sample of which is illustrated in Appendix 4. Please note that this registration form can be used whether or not you intend to obtain computer statistics. For further information contact the author at SFU.

Subjective Evaluation Techniques

While objective methods will give you the vital quantitative data — the facts & figures — subjective methods can give you qualitative information — how people feel about the program. Intramurals are for *everybody* in the school, so people's feelings are important. Some techniques you can use are:
1. Surveys & questionnaires
2. Participant feedback
3. Suggestion boxes
4. Meetings with all committees at end of year
5. Meeting with Intramurals Council at end of year
6. Feedback from officials
7. Feedback from teachers
8. Criticism

SAFETY AND LEGAL LIABILITY

Safety

In any physical activity program accidents and injuries are an unfortunate possibility. The frequently lower level of both fitness and skill of intramural sports participants, as compared with interscholastic athletes, may be a contributory factor in injury situations. Accidents are likely to occur for the following reasons:
1. Inadequate fitness level for certain activities
2. Lack of medical information on participants, including previous injuries
3. Too many games in a short space of time
4. Low skill level
5. Unequal competition
6. Too competitive atmosphere
7. Inadequate officiating or supervision
8. Faulty equipment or extraneous equipment on playing surface
9. Normal risks inherent in certain sports, especially contact sports

The staff advisor is responsible for minimizing the possibility of injuries through preventive actions. All of the above factors are preventable to a large degree by using a mixture of common sense and the following guidelines:
1. Conditioning prior to start of activity

2. Medical clearance or report with contraindications noted
3. Scheduling Committee controls frequency of games
4. Raise skill level through clinics
5. Selection Committee attempts to equalize competition
6. Employ A and B League system together with counselling by staff advisor when necessary
7. Proper supervision of every event, and Referees Committee responsible for training officials
8. Discontinue points for participation if necessary
9. Equipment regularly checked by equipment managers and staff advisor; and all unnecessary equipment removed from playing area
10. Activities and Rules Committee modify rules to minimize body contact and enforce mandatory use of protective equipment where appropriate

In addition, all school, district, and governmental safety guidelines and accident regulations should be known and strictly adhered to by everyone involved in the program.

Legal Liability

As for legal liability, ascertain your position by consulting the appropriate person(s) in your school district. Be sure you understand your scope of duty, plus what is covered by the school district's insurance policy and under what circumstances. Safeguard yourself as you would your students.

CHAPTER VI
Programming

Activities
Scheduling
Playdays

ACTIVITIES

A well balanced intramural sports program should contain a variety of individual, dual and team activities, plus special events. Some of the factors that the Activities & Rules Committee should consider when choosing activities for the school year are highlighted below.

1. Select activities on the basis of the season of year and other prevailing conditions (e.g. pool, no gym, limited equipment, etc.).
2. Select activities according to the needs and interests of students (e.g. a paper airplane contest for 'intellectuals'). The important thing here is offering something for everyone.
3. Include at least a few activities which require little skill and which the emphasis is on the enjoyment, as opposed to the competitive, aspects of play.
4. Selection may be based on the results of a questionnaire administered by the Activities & Rules Committee.
5. Prominence should be given to activities which have implications for lifetime living (carryover sports).
6. Activities should be presented in a progressive manner from Kindergarten to Grade 12.
7. Activities for the elementary grades should be selected with special attention to the child's ability.
8. Activities introduced in P.E. classes can be followed up by intramural sports programming scheduling. This method also helps to publicize

and generate enthusiasm for the intramural sports program.
9. Coed activities should be selected whenever possible.
10. Select activities which generally do not require special equipment or lengthy training periods to get students in shape for the activity.
11. If Fall weather is good, don't start indoor intramurals while the students want to play outside. Be prepared to start your indoors program at the first drop of rain!
12. Some activities will be less popular than others. Efforts must be made to educate students in some of these activities, otherwise they will want to play floor hockey all year.
13. League activities should be of short duration, say a maximum of 3 weeks for one activity. Finish up while the students want more.

SCHEDULING

The prime objective in scheduling is to achieve the greatest amount of playing time for the greatest number of students while retaining administrative simplicity. There are several possibilities open to the Scheduling Committee:
1. Round Robin
2. Single Knock-out
3. Consolation
4. Double Knock-out
5. Ladder and Pyramid Tournament
6. "Organized" Free Play
7. Special Events
Most schools use all of the above scheduling methods. The advantages/disadvantages of each method are highlighted below.

Round Robin

1. Undoubtedly the best system for league activities.
2. All teams play each other once resulting in the most valid champion.
3. As a quick aid to scheduling, use the Scheduling Sheet in Appendix 3.

Single Knock-Out

1. This scheduling method does not satisfy our prime objective since half the participants will play only once.
2. For large numbers of entries or limited time available to run the league/tournament, this method may be the only way. If possible, however, utilize the consolation method.
3. Reference should be made to the texts for logistics (Appendix 1).

Consolation

1. This method is similar to single knock-out except that all first-round losers take part in a consolation, single knock-out tournament.
2. All participants are guaranteed at least two games.

Double Knock-Out

1. Almost identical to the consolation method, except that the winner of the "losers" bracket (or consolation round) has a chance to win the whole tournament.
2. Participants must lose twice before elimination so this results in a more valid champion than in single knock-out.
3. More cumbersome and time consuming to set up.
4. Double knock-out tournaments should never be scheduled for outdoor events (unless the weather can be guaranteed!)
5. Reference should be made to the texts for logistics (Appendix 1).

Ladder and Pyramid Tournament

1. This challenge system is ideal for activities such as badminton and table tennis.
2. The winner is the student placed at the top of the ladder or pyramid at the end of a set period of time, say 6 weeks.
3. This system requires constant vigilance. Stipulations regarding minimum number of games per week participant must be made and adhered to.
4. To keep these tournaments moving, start the best players on the bottom of the ladder or pyramid. Generally their self-esteem will cause them to play regularly to work their way up to the top.
5. Refer to the texts for logistics (Appendix 1).

"Organized" Free Play

This concept can be introduced to reduce competitiveness. Thus, one day per week may be set aside for an activity (which is changed every week and advertised well in advance). Students merely show up and teams are organized, if necessary, on an ad hoc basis.

Special Events

1. These are novelty events, held on a one-shot basis either in the evening, on the weekend or during regular school hours and scheduled at various times so that all students will have a chance to participate.
2. They should be held at least once a month.
3. If handled well they can have a very positive promotional effect.

Useful Aids in Scheduling

N = number of entries
1. N−1 determines the number of games in a single knock-out tournament
2. 2N−1 determines the maximum number of games in a double knock-out tournament (the number is one less than this if the winner of the "winners" division remains undefeated)
3. $\dfrac{N(N-1)}{2}$ determines the number of games in a round robin competition

Some Other Important Points in Scheduling

1. Keep leagues short (maximum of 3 weeks).
2. Remember to schedule around holidays.
3. In tournaments, proper placement of seeded playes and byes is important. Refer to the texts for logistics.

PLAYDAYS

The concept of Interschool Intramurals, or playdays, is gaining popularity at all levels of the educational system. It involves taking intramural champion teams (or select teams, or teams consisting of interested students) in a number of different activities to another school for competition.
1. Playdays can be scheduled for after school, or, preferably, on a weekend.
2. Low key competition is emphasized.
3. Simultaneous organization of a picnic involving parents adds to the enjoyment of the event.
4. Spectators are encouraged, thereby fostering school spirit.
5. This type of activity provides added incentive and extra fun for non-athletes.
6. The concept can be expanded to include more than two schools.

CHAPTER VII

Games

Net Games
Running Games
Batting Games
Aquatics Games

The following sample games and activities are presented for the benefit of the reader. Frankly, the only basic limitation to structuring enjoyable activities for inclusion in the intramural sports program is the imagination of the program coordinator.

So don't delay any longer. Evaluate your situation and develop your program. Remember that *at all times* the emphasis should be on *fun!* (Author's note: we are extremely grateful for the assistance of our colleagues M. Hardisty and R. Lindstrom for their assistance in writing this chapter and developing the games presented herein.)

NET & COURT GAMES

Lead up to VOLLEYBALL

1. Newcomb

No. of Players:	6-9 players arranged in lines on each side of the net.
Skills:	Throwing and catching.
Equipment:	A large ball.
Play:	The game starts with the right hand player in the rear line throwing the ball over the net. The player catching the ball throws it right back. Play continues until the ball drops to the floor on one side or is thrown out of bounds. The non-offending team scores a point. The offending team puts the ball into play again, as at the beginning of the game.
	Players may rotate their positions by lines at the end of a time limit, or given number of points. Normal volleyball-type rotation may also be introduced as a teaching measure, when points are given up.
Variation:	A light medicine ball (weighted) can be used for added "exercise" value.

2. Volleycom

Volleycom is very much like Newcomb except that the "volley" feature is utilized. Instead of catching the ball after it clears the net, the player must "volley" it once toward a team member who catches the ball and then throws it over the net. Two players are therefore involved in each rally—one receiving the ball with a volley, and the other catching and throwing.

As players improve, a second and perhaps third "volley" or hit can be introduced—before the ball is caught and returned with a throw over the net. The object at all times is sustained action.

3. Deck Tennis

Court:	Singles — 12' x 40' or 10' x 30'. Doubles — 18' x 40' or (centre line 9')
Net:	Height — 4'9" or use regular net height for volleyball.
Equipment:	2—5' posts One net—1½" wide Ring—7" in diameter, rubber (or rope).
Object of Game:	One team or side tries to throw the ring over the net to touch the floor on the other side (opposite).
Rules:	i) Game consists of 15 points. Play best 2 out of 3 games to determine a winner.

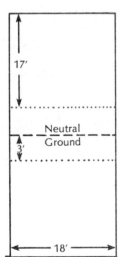

ii) Any ring falling on a line is considered in bounds
iii) Any ring falling in legal play area after hitting the net is considered a good return—a served ring which touches the top of the net and is otherwise good should be 're-served' without penalty.
iv) Score as badminton—player may score only during serve. Server continues changing sides as long as she scores. If a point is lost or opponents score, serve is lost and opponents serve (back right side). In doubles, players change sides when starting to serve with the 'last' server receiving.
v) Ring must be caught in one hand only. If two players catch it, one must release hand for the return throw.
vi) The delivery of the ring be made with an UPWARD movement and must rise at least 6" after leaving the hand. Over-hand constitutes loss of a point.
vii) Ring must pass over the net and is considered grounded where it first strikes, not where it rolls. Neutral ground on each side of the net is 3 feet wide. Players may not step within this area nor may the ring be grounded there.
viii) Any player may not take more than steps with the ring. Ring must be returned from the position in the court where it is caught and the return must be made immediately.

N.B. This may be played in teams—in volleyball formation.

4. Barrage Ball

Skills:	Throwing and catching
Players:	An even number of team, 8-10 players.
Equipment:	Volleyball net, uneven number (e.g., 7) of volleyball or playground balls per game.

Games

Rules:	Two teams face each other across the net. The balls are divided unevenly. The aim of the game is to throw the balls to the opponent as quickly as possible. At any given time when a whistle is blown, the team with the smallest number of balls scores. Periods should not be more than two minutes.
Variation:	As players develop skill, balls may be served and volleyed.

5. Nebraska Ball

Formation:	Arrange players in a scattered formation on each side of the net.
Equipment:	Volleyball court, net, 4-inch ball.
No. of Players:	10 to 15 on each team.
Skills:	Serving and volleying.
Play:	1. One player serves the ball over the net from a serving line drawn fifteen feet from the net. 2. Any number of players may hit the ball to assist it over the net. 3. A point is scored when the ball lands on the floor.
Teaching Suggestions:	Shorten serving distances if skill level is too low.

6. Bounce Volleyball

Skills:	Serving, rotation, volleying.
Players:	10-12, two teams.
Equipment:	Volleyball and volleyball net.
Rules:	The ball is served from behind the service line. An assist is permitted. The player continues to serve until he makes an error, or his team fails to return the ball to the opponents' court. The ball must bounce once when it crosses the net before it is hit. Any number of players may hit it, but no player may contact it twice in succession. Only the serving may score as in volleyball. After side out, players rotate.

Server (rotates to ■).

The winner may be decided at the end of a set period (e.g., 10 minutes, or 15 pts. may constitute a game).

7. Shower Volleyball

Formation:	Arrange players in scattered formation on each side of net.
Equipment:	Volleyball and net.
No. of Players:	10 to 12 on each team.
Skills:	Volleying.
Play:	1. Two teams of equal numbers on each side of the net. 2. Play is started by one player batting the ball over the net. 3. Any player on the opposite side attempts to catch the ball. 4. The player who catches it is allowed one step then he must hit it back over the net.

41

5. One point for the serving team if the receiving team does not catch the ball.

6. One point for receiving team if they catch the ball before it bounces.

Teaching Suggestions: As skill improves, have each child throw the ball up then hit it over the net.

8. Modified Volleyball

Skills: Serving, setting-up, volleying.

Players: Any number up to 12 on a team.

Equipment: Volleyball court, net (at 6'6''), volleyball.

Rules: Teams volley the ball back and forth over the net, trying to place the ball so that the opponents cannot return it. The ball may be served from any position in the rear half of the court, and an assist is permitted. Any number of players may contact the ball before it is sent over the net. Players rotate as in Bounce Volleyball. Only the serving side scores. The game may be played in two ten-minute periods, or 15 points may consititute a game.

Modification: For younger children, use beachball or balloons.

Lead up to TENNIS

1. Paddle Tennis

No. of Players: Two for singles, four for doubles.

Equipment: Tennis or rubber ball (6 in. playground ball may be used), 2-4 wooden paddles, badminton net (piece of line with white strips of cloth tied to it may be used).

Area: Gymnasium, or outside area with hard surface such as cement, asphalt, wood or clay. Net 2'10'' high at center, 3'1'' at posts. For younger children, 2'2''.

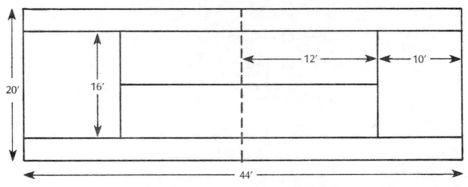

Directions: The game is played and scored as lawn tennis except for the serve, which is underhand. Only one serve is allowed to put the ball in play for each point. Beginners may have two serves if needed.

The server stands in the right corner behind the baseline and serves the ball over the centre line to the player diagonally opposite him on the other side. The opposing player returns the ball, and the game con tinues until one of the players or teams fails to return it. The server then changes to the left side of the court and serves. When a player or team fails to return a ball, a score is made by the opponents. If a ball is hit out of bounds or fails to cross the centre line, a score is also made by the opponents.

Scoring: Points are scored as in tennis: 15, 30, 40, game. If both teams have a score of 40-40, the score is called "deuce", and play continues until one team wins two consecutive points. The game may also be scored as in table tennis with the player who first made 21 points being declared the winner. When the game is scored in this manner, the server alternates with the receiver after every 5 points.

Variation: May be played with the hands instead of with paddles, game called "Hand Tennis".

2. Floor Tennis

The great appeal of this game is the opportunity to return hard drives and smashes since the celluloid ball loses some of its speed on the longer court. The ball thus remains in play over a longer period of time.

Playing Court: 16 feet long by 8 feet wide, divided lengthwise and crosswise in the middle, thus making four sections 8 feet by 4 feet.

Net: 21 inches high by 9 feet long including any supports used at the bottom to anchor the net without side supports.

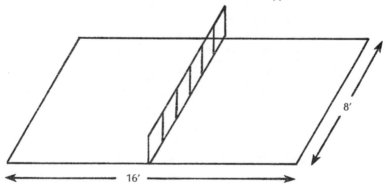

8'

16'

Equipment: The bat and ball are larger and heavier than table tennis equipment.

Rules: They are the same as table tennis except:
1. The serve is made from the server's right hand court to the receiver's right hand court starting with a bounce behind the base line.
2. Serving stroke must be made no higher than the waist.
3. Balls hitting on the lines are good.
4. A serve which touches the net, and is otherwise good, is a let serve and the point is replayed.
5. Scoring the same as in table tennis.

Note: Instead of buying the proper equipment, use a badminton court, old tennis ball, paddleball paddles, and fix the badminton net low on its posts.

Lead up to BADMINTON

1. Goodminton

Positions:

Rotate in the direction of the arrows—

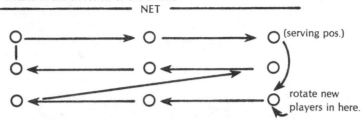

Service:
A service involves putting the bird in play by the player in the right forward position by batting the bird over the net into the opposing team's court. The bird must be struck below the waist with an underhand service.

Server has one serve only. The bird must clear the net entirely.

Other Rules:
1. The bird must be clearly batted; scooping, lifting, shoving, or following the bird shall be considered as holding.
2. The bird may be batted in any direction.
3. The bird, other than on the service, may be recovered from the net provided the player avoids touching the net.
4. The bird may be batted only three times by one team before being returned over the net. (The same player may not hit the bird twice in succession, but he may give the first and third hit.)

Points:
Points can only be scored by the team serving. If the other team fails to return the bird, the serving team scores one point. If the serving team fails to get the bird back to the other team, then the other team first rotates and then serves.

2. 3 Man Badminton

Equipment:
Same as regular badminton

Rules:
Each team consists of 3 players — these can be all boys, all girls, or mixed. The rules are the same as in regular badminton doubles, except players on each team must hit the bird consecutively, in strict rotation.

RUNNING GAMES

DODGEBALL GAMES

1. Medical War Ball

Break your gym class into two teams. One person on each team is designated as the doctor; all others are soldiers. The object is for one team to eliminate all of the soldiers and the doctor from the opposing team. Each team goes to one end of the gym or play area. Five rubber balls are placed on the center line equal distance from each team. One small space at each end of the playing area is designated as the hospital.

At the sound of a whistle all of the members of both teams, except the doctor, run for the center of the gym and try to get one of the rubber balls and carry it back behind the end line. As soon as all of the balls have been taken behind the end lines they may be thrown at any opposing soldier. When anyone is hit by a ball in the air (if a ball bounces it does not count as a hit), he must fall down exactly where he has been hit. The job of the doctor is to sneak out and drag any of the wounded soldiers to the hospital. If he gets the soldier back without being hit himself, the soldier may re-enter the war. If the doctor is hit he also falls where he is hit and no one else can be rescued. The game, however, continues until all of the soldiers from a team have been eliminated. Teams then change sides, balls are put back into the center, a new doctor is picked, and the game starts over again.

Diagram for Medical War Ball

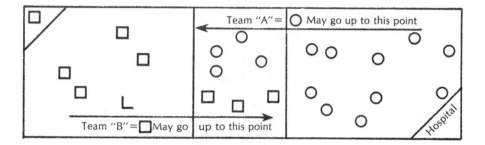

2. War Ball

Rules:

1. A player is eliminated when:
   a) he is hit on or below the knees by a "live ball" (a thrown ball that has not bounced twice, hit a wall or eliminated another player already).
   b) he, in attempting to catch a "live ball", drops it.
   c) he goes into the opponent's zone to play a ball.
   d) he kneels down to make it almost impossible for an opponent to hit him on or below the knees.
   e. he blocks a "live ball" with his arms.
2. A player may block a "live ball" with another ball. However, if in doing this, the ball is knocked out of his hands, he is out.
3. There should be six to eight volleyballs in the game.
4. A player with the ball can move anywhere in his zone or the free zone.
5. A player in possession of the ball must be encouraged to throw the ball as quickly as they can.
6. Play the game until there are six or eight players left on either team. At this point have the teams change ends. The team lined up first receives all of the balls to start the next game.
7. Starting positions for the game...see diagram.

Variations:

Player is out when hit directly below the waist, rather than on the first bounce.

45

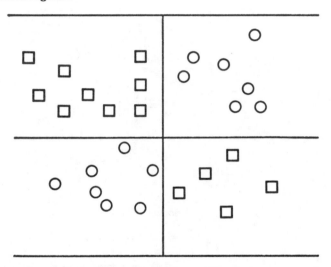

3. Quadrant Dodgeball

A square or circular field is divided into quadrants by two perpendicular lines through the center. Players are in two equal teams and each team is itself divided, not necessarily equally, between two of the quadrants. The teams alternate in the quadrants, so that the parts of one team are in diagonally opposite quadrants. Each team has a ball with which it tries to hit the opponents. Only direct hits count, and only one hit can be counted from one throw. Any player may move from one to the other of his team's quadrants at any time. Play is continued for a set time and the numbers of hits compared.

Variation: A man who is hit is eliminated. The game continues until all of one team are out.

4. German Dodgeball (Dead or Alive, Spy Dodgeball)

The court is divided in half, with a second line 4′ to 6′ from each end wall. The players are scattered on their own side of the center line with one player from each team stationed behind the opposite team. He is the first "spy" and his only function is to return the ball to his own team if it comes to him across the end line. The object of the game is to eliminate the opponents by striking them below the shoulders with a thrown playball. When hit, a player goes behind the opposite end line — his is dead and becomes a "spy". These "spies" may try to eliminate the opponents by attacking from the rear. The first "spy" is still alive and may return once to his team to be eliminated as soon as he is joined by another "spy".

46

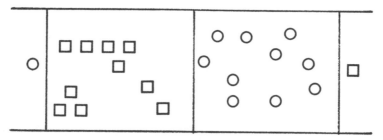

The game starts with a toss-up at center between two opposing players. If the ball hits the floor first and then a player, he is not out and any player may pick it up and throw. A live player may save his own life by catching a thrown ball. If he tries to catch it but drops it, he is out. He may also save the life of a teammate by catching a ball that bounces off him, provided that the ball is caught before it strikes the floor. If he drops it, they are both out. If a thrown ball strikes two players and then the floor, they are both out. If a live player steps over the center line or the line behind his team, he is out. If a "spy" steps over the restraining line and retrieves the ball for his team, he must return it to the opponents.

The game ends when all the players of one team have been eliminated. When the players have become proficient, a second ball may be added.

5. Jail Ball

Area: Gym—with one restraining line on each end.

Game: One team is on each side of centre.
                       Each team has one large utility ball to begin the game.
                       The object is to hit a member of the opposing team below the waist.
                       Only direct hits count.

Jail: Area behind the opposition's restraining line. A player must go to jail
                       for the following:
                       1) Hit by a legally thrown ball (if below the waist).
                       2) Throwing a ball which hits a player above the waist.
                       3) Stepping into the opponents territory.
                       4) Attempting to catch but fumbling a ball thrown by an opponent.

47

Players in jail may throw balls which come into their area and if they hit an opponent he must also go to jail.

Scoring: When all players of one team are in jail the other team is awarded one point.

The game then begins over.

6. Traditional Circle Game

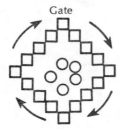

Eliminated if hit below the waist or for stepping on the outside circle line or intentionally knocking the ball down. Outside players must have one foot on or behind the line. A ball inside the circle is "alive" at all times.

Variation: The ball must bounce once before it counts as a hit, so as to reduce power balls.

7. Gate Dodgeball

Gate

The game is played the same as Dodge Ball except that a gate composed of two markers such as badminton stands are placed in the outside of the circle among the throwers. The instructor stands beside the gate and acts as a counter.

All on the inside of the circle hit by a ball must immediately exit through the gate and run once around the outside returning through the gate to rejoin the game. The team having the lesser number going through the gate wins.

French and English

Apparatus: 12-20 tokens (bean bags, skittles, flags, etc.)

The ground is divided into halves by a central line, and a base line running parallel to this is drawn across each end. The tokens are divided and laid out at equal distances behind the base lines. The players divide into two teams which form up along their own base lines. When the game is started, players attempt to traverse their opponent's territory and cross their base lines without being touched. Any player who succeeds in doing this carries back one enemy token which he places behind his own base line. A successful player may not be touched on his return journey. If a player is touched while on his opponent's half of the ground, he becomes a prisoner and must remain behind his opponent's base line until a prisoner from his own side succeeds in crossing the base line, thus freeing him. Both players are then granted safe passage back to their own territory. When a player is touched, his captors must accompany him back to the base line. When a captor is freed, both he and the player who freed him must return to their side of the central line before engaging in the game.

The winning team is the team which captures the whole of the tokens or the game may be decided on points, 1 point for each prisoner, 2 for token.

Kabaddi (from India for 10 or more players)

Two equal teams stand on either side of dividing line and 20-30 feet from that line. The line may be indicated by a rope or rocks or a lime marker. A player from Team One approaches and crosses the dividing line into Team Two's territory, calling out, "Kabaddi, Kabaddi, Kabaddi!" (pronounced Kabaddee with accent on last syllable). He goes as close as he can to the members of Team Two, trying to touch anyone of them with his hand or foot and at the same time avoid being seized by him. If he succeeds in touching an opponent and in getting back across the dividing line without being seized, the player he has touched must drop out of the game. However, he must continue to call "Kabaddi!" all the time he is trying to tag an opponent. To make it more difficult, this must all be done in one breath. If he is successful in his efforts and finds he is running out of breath, he must run back to his side of the line. If his opponents should seize him, he may struggle to get back to the dividing line. If he is successful in reaching it with either his hand or his foot, he is safe and the opponent who first seized him drops out of the game. After a player on Team One has gone over into Team Two's territory and returns to his side or has been captured, a player from Team Two ventures into Team One's territory. The game continues until one side has no players left.

Hurly Burly (exhilarating game on field with few regulations)

The players divide into two teams and arrange themselves in their own half of the ground. Goals are clearly marked by posts, chairs, or chalk lines. Goal: side and halfway lines can be added as the need arises. The aim of each team is to get the ball through the opponent's goal or over their goal line. The players are free to propel the ball as they like, provided there is no pushing or rough play. They may kick, bat with the open hand, throw, head or fist the ball from one to another, run with, bounce or dribble it along with foot or hand. Players must pass when touched while holding the ball. The players will quickly grasp that the game is a passing one in which the ball should move about the field from one player to another.

Size of pitch: not more than 60 yds. by 30 yds.

7-10 players per team.

Saddlebags (Native Indian)

This game is like lacrosse but does not require expensive equipment. In place of a lacrosse ball, two beanbags are used. The bags are fastened together with a band of cloth about two feet long. A strong stick than resembles a hockey stick is carried by each player. The bags are handled by the sticks since it is against the rules of the game to touch the bags with hands or feet. Rough play of any sort is not allowed. The bags may be caught in the air, picked from the ground or carried toward the goal. Also the bags may be thrown from the stick high in the air towards the goal.

The playing areas are called the prairies and they are about the size of a football field. The goals at each end of the field are made of two upright posts and a crossbar 10 ft. from the ground. The players are divided into tribes called the braves (backs) and the bucks (goal-keepers). The captain of each team is known as the chief.

The chiefs toss for choice of goal of first case and then place their men in their respective places. The play is started by the chief of one of the tribes taking the bag on his stick and tossing it as far as he can towards the opponents goal. One of the opposing braves tries to catch the bags on his stick. If he succeeds he then runs for the goal or passes the bag on to a teammate as in American football. The opposing team may lift the bags from the stick of the runner or catch them as they are in the air, provided the runner's stick or person is not touched. The fair method of securing the bags from the runner is to slip the end of the stick under the bags and lift them off.

The scoring of the game is as follows: one scalp for running over the goal line with the bags; three scalps for throwing the bags under the crossbars; ten scalps for throwing the bags over the goal posts. When a score is not made, play is started from the centre with the side that did not score having the cast. When the bags are thrown out of bounds, the umpire throws them in where they went out, and the players on both teams stand in the places where they were when the bags crossed the boundary line.

Ball Play (Native Indian)

It was a strenuous game when played by Indian braves, because of the large playing area and the absence of rest periods. Each side has its goal 250 paces from the middle of the field. The goal posts were 6 ft. apart and 6 ft. high with a cross bar on top.

The Indians had umpires who were usually the old men of the tribe, and their chief duty seemed to be to watch the articles that were being wagered by the enthusiastic spectators.

The players were divided into two sides with a captain each. One of the umpires started the game by tossing the ball in the air, and the players of both sides rushed to catch it. As soon as a player caught the ball, he threw it toward the opponent's goal. An alert opponent rushed to catch it and send it back. The players were allowed to snatch or knock the ball from another's hands. The game continued until one side had thrown the ball through the opponent's goal. After a goal the ball was immediately thrown back by the side that did not score, instead of being carried back to the center as in most ball games of this type. The team that threw the ball between the opponent's goal 100 times was the winner. The Indians were so skillful and alert that they played a very fast game.

It was a ball game of this type that was used as a disguise before the terrible massacre at Fort Mackinaw, which took place after the French and Indian War, during the Pontiac conspiracy.

Field Ball

Field Ball is played outdoors on a relatively large field, the size appropriate to the number playing and the players aerobic condition. If there are 10 to 15 players on a side, a regulation football field may be used. Smaller or larger areas can be used depending on your inclination. (We once used an area 180 yds. by 100 yds. for a pre-season track workout). The teacher, with experience, will be able to adjust the field size to get maximum aerobic training benefits without losing the competitive structure of the game. As in Non-Stop Ball, the field has boundaries, but there is no out-of-bounds. The ball, usually a soccer ball, is always in play. Play continues when the ball goes over the boundaries. Scores, counting one point each, are made when the attacking team gains possession of the ball in their opponent's goal area. The goal area is the area directly behind the end boundary lines, extending back indefinitely. The ball, put in play at the centre line at the beginning of the game and after each score, can be advanced in any way possible: running, throwing, passing, kicking, dribbling, air dribbling and by any other innovation. The advance is stopped only when an opposing player tags the player with possession of the ball with one hand (as in "one hand anywhere"). The tagged player must immediately back off five to six yards from the player who tagged him and throw the ball. Play immediately continues on the change of possession. It is crucial that this exchange take place without delay. If an official is available, there is no problem in managing the game. If not, the continuity of the game depends on the spirit of the players to call their own game fairly. It should be notd that a player must actually have possession of the ball to be stopped. If he is in the midst of dribbling, air dribbling, or kicking, he cannot be stopped.

To reiterate, a score is made when a player has possession of the ball in the other team's

The basic component in planning the program of intramural activities is the imagination of the program director.

goal area. He can run into the area with the ball from in-bounds or from out-of-bounds. He can receive a pass or retrieve a kicked ball or the like. Just about any reasonable way of getting the ball there is acceptable. If the defensive team recovers a loose ball in their own goal area, they cannot be tagged until they bring the ball back over their own end line. From that point on, they may be tagged.

Some points of strategy might be valuable. Players with the ball should try at all costs to avoid getting caught with the ball. If they are about to be tagged, they should get rid of the ball, preferably advancing it forward. Defensively, either a man-to-man or zone type defensive may be employed, with players spread rather evenly over the whole field. In general, the game is extremely fast moving. Scorers are not particularly difficult to make. All players have a chance to become fully involved, handling the ball and creating a wide variety of play situations. Air dribbling, feinting, fast breaks, long sprints, jump passes, running kicks and the like are characteristic of the race-horse pace of the game. There is a minimal amount of body contact, making it a relatively safe game. It is for those who love to run and handle the ball without restriction.

Three Steps

Three steps is played with a junior football. The playing field, sixty or more feet long, is marked with side boundary lines and goal lines. From two to ten players form each of two teams. The ball is passed by each team in turn, and whenever the ball is passed over the opponent's goal line, a point is scored.

The two teams are on opposite ends of the field defending their own goal line. The game is started by a player from either team, selected by chance. Upon the signal from the referee, he passes the ball from his own goal line toward the opponents' goal. The opponents attempt to catch the pass. If the pass is caught by the opponents, the catcher is permitted to move three steps toward the opponents' goal, and he passes from that spot attempting to score. However, if the pass is not caught by the receiving team, it must be passed by the player who first touched it after it hit the ground and from the spot where he first touched it. The players on the offensive team must forfeit the pass when any team member does not stay in line with the passer, or behind the passer until the ball is passed.

Whenever a ball goes over a side boundary line before it is touched by a player on the receiving team, it is recovered by a near-by player on the receiving team and played from a spot three steps inside the boundary line at the point where the ball went out of bounds.

Play is continuous with each team passing (offensive) and receiving (defensive) alternately until one team scores, or succeeds in passing the ball over the opponents' goal line. After a score is made, the ball is put into play by the team scored against from its goal line. The length of the playing period is determined by the players before the game is started. The team which scores the most points within the playing time wins the game.

Scoring: 3 pts. are awarded for throwing the ball over the opponents' goal posts. 1 pt. is awarded for throwing the ball over the opponents' goal line and the ball is not caught. If the ball is caught no point is awarded and the defending team may move the ball up to their goal line to throw the ball towards their opponents.

Teaching Suggestions:

Limit play to passing; or to punting; or permit both passing or punting.

Permit players to adapt football rules and scoring to their game or to originate suitable rules; but, *do not permit,* for elementary school players, any tackling, blocking, tripping, or other play which involves body contact.

Change the number of steps permitted if the game is slow; children often play the game as Five Steps, Six Steps, *et cetera*.

Team A—□
Defensive

Team B—○
Offensive

Team B
Goal Line

○
○
○
○
○
○

□   □

□   □

□   □

Goal Line
Team A

Lead up to SOCCER

1. Hand Soccer

Modified Rules:	
Organization:	Six players on each side: 1 goalie, 2 backs, 3 forwards.
Equipment:	1 small colored plastic ball; 2 gym benches placed on sides.
Rules:	1. Ball handling — ball must be hit with the OPEN HAND. It cannot be held or grabbed or thrown. 2. The ball may *NOT be kicked.* Players may BLOCK with their feet only. 3. The ball may be HEADED.
To Start Game:	Teams line up on or behind white line. Referee throws ball up over centre spot. Teams move forward. AFTER EACH GOAL, COMMENCE GAME THIS WAY.
Infractions & Penalties:	1. Holding, grabbing, kicking the ball are the most common infractions. A team which commits one of these MINOR FOULS has a FREE SHOT CALLED AGAINST IT. Opposing team places ball on *centre spot* (N.B. ALL OTHER PLAYERS MUST STAND BEHIND THE BALL) and one player shoots at goal. 2. Tripping, charging, fighting, etc., are MAJOR FOULS. A team which commits a major foul has a PENALTY SHOT AWARDED AGAINST IT. Ball is placed on penalty spot (ALL OTHER PLAYERS MUST BE BEHIND THE BALL), and *one* player shoots.
Face-Off Circles:	Use only when the progress of the game has been SLOWED DOWN. 1. The ball frozen against the wall under a pile of bodies warrants a whistle. Go to nearest face-off circle. One member of each team in circle with you. Throw ball up to re-start game. 2. Use face-off circle when a goalie lies on the ball, protecting it. 3. Use face-off circle if any form of injury occurs.
Duration:	Five minutes each way is ideal. Teams change ends at half-time. This is an exhaustive game. Halves should not exceed seven minutes.

2. Crab Soccer or Black Bottom

Players:	Any number divided into 2 teams.
Equipment:	Soccer ball, volleyball, or playball.

Area: Suitable for gymnasium, playroom or playground.

Rules: Each team is given one end of the gym to defend. Players must sit in the 'crab' position (hands and feet on the floor, seat toward floor). The seat may be rested on the floor. Each team has a goaler who is the only player allowed to stand. Only the goaler may use his hands; other players may only kick the ball with their feet or head it with their heads. The penalty for an infraction — ball is awarded to opponents. Game begins with a face-off in the middle and continues until one side scores a goal by kicking or heading it past the goaler. If the goaler makes a save, he may throw or kick the ball to teammate. A goaler's crease should be established. Also, a set height for the goal should be decided upon. The whole width of the gym is usually the goal area. The ball may be out of bounds. For a more complicated after school game, forward and defencemen can be introduced with off sides, penalty box, free kicks, etc.

Scoring: One point for each goal scored.

Variation: The game can be played without a goaler and the ball must be *rolled* across the goal line to score a point.

3. Modified Soccer

The objective of the game is to make a score by kicking the ball across the opponent's goal line. Use feet, legs, or body. Rotate players after each score. End zone players must stay in end zone. To score, ball must cross goal line even with the shoulder.

End
Zone

4. Speedball

Playing Area: Soccer (or football) field.

Equipment: Soccer (or rugby) ball.

Players: Can vary from 6 to 15.

Rules: 1. A ball on the ground must be played with the feet as in soccer.
2. On catching a fly ball (one that has not touched the ground since it was last played) the player may:
a) run with it
b) pass it
c) punt it or drop kick it if you are in your own end
d) play it as in soccer

3. To stop a player running with the ball, the defense merely touches him below the waist (or tackles him). When touched the player must immediately drop the ball. As soon as it *touches the ground,* it becomes replayable (by any one other than the man who dropped it.)

4. Out of bounds on side; soccer throw in.

5. Out of bounds on end; throw, punt or place kick.

Scoring: 3 pts. for a touchdown (try). The ball must be run over.

2 pts. for a drop kick.

1 pt. for a soccer style goal.

5. Line Soccer

Players are divided into two teams and are lined up on their own goal lines. At a signal, one player from each team (extreme right ends) run to the center while referee drops the ball. The objective of the game is to kick ball over opponent's line. Linesmen may use hands to stop ball but cannot throw it — roll it in.

Head and Pass

Playing Area: Gymnasium

No. per Side: 5 to 11; depending on the size of the playing area.

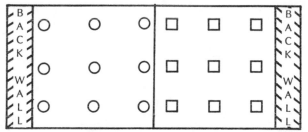

line 8' high   half-way line   line 8' high

Object of Game: The object of the game is to head the ball against the opponent's wall within an 8' limit. An approach of alternate head and hand passing has to be used.

Fouls occur when: A ball is headed twice in succession

A ball is handled twice in succession

**The above two points apply in all cases

Opposition must *intercept* in an alternate manner.

A thrown ball hits the ground (it must be headed on the fly)

To Start Game: To begin the game or restart following a score, the ball is thrown from a player on the halfway line *back* to the head of a fellow team member.

Note: Try to encourage the "short pass and head" approach rather than continuous use of long throws. A volleyball is ideal to use in this game.

INDOOR SOCCER RULES

1. Number of Players: each team can have up to 9 players with no more than 5 on the floor at any given time.

2. Length of Game: two 20 minute halves with 5 minute break.

3. Substitution: a team can freely substitute players throughout the game. The referee *must* be notified prior to a goalkeeper substitution.

4. Scoring: a goal can be scored from any area of the court other than the goalkeeper's area.

5. Goalkeeper's Area: this area should be clearly marked. This area is out of bounds to all members of the attacking team. If an attacking player is carried into this area on his own momentum *after* he has played the ball, he is not penalized. The goalkeeper is not allowed to handle the ball outside this area.

6. Body Contact: there will be a minimum of body contact. The referee has authority to ban all players for rough or dangerous play.

7. High Ball: ball must be below head height unless deflected. This is left to the discretion of the referee.

8. Throw-Ins and Corners: under-arm throw-in only, including goalie, subject to high ball rule.

9. Penalties: penalties are given for infringements of the above rules and also for tripping, handling the ball, etc. All penalties are indirect free kicks. When the free kick is taken, the penalized team must stand 2 yards from the ball. A penalty goal may be awarded if a player is brought down with only the goalkeeper to beat.
   The referee may eject players for 5 minutes for serious rule infringements. The player may re-enter the game if a goal is scored against his team during the 5 minute penalty.

10. The ball can be played off the side walls but it is out of play on touching the end walls where it becomes either a goalie's ball or a corner.

Suggestions

1. Goals should be of sturdy design and we recommend the following dimensions:

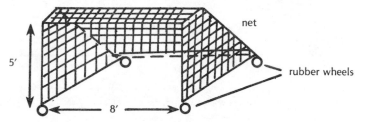

2. Goalkeeper's area should be appropriate to size of gym and size of goals. for the above goal measurements, the area should be:

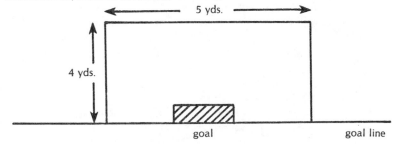

Games

Lead up to BASKETBALL

1. European or Team Handball

Court:

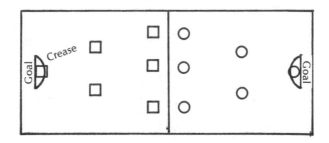

Equipment:	Two goals 1 playball (8″) or volleyball
Rules:	1. No dribbling
	2. Allowed 3 steps before passing
	3. Must keep out of crease at all time (Penalty - other teams ball)
	4. Must not use your feet (only hands)
	5. Must not foul man (same as basketball)
	6. Free throw if fouled (defence back up 10 yards)
	7. Goalie cannot come out of crease
	8. If ball out of bounds at ends — goalie's ball
	9. May throw with one or two hands
	10. Start game with jump ball at centre and after a score
Players:	6 from each team at one time (3 forwards, 2 defencement, 1 goalie) — others sub in, using platoon system if possible.

2. Bucketball

Players:	6 players per team, 3 forwards, 1 bucket holder
Rules:	The ball can only be moved around the floor by passing The ball cannot be carried more than one step The bucket holder must hold the bucket (garbage can) with two hands and remain on the chair

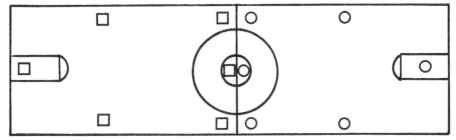

No player except the bucket holder is allowed in the square of the key
No shots can be taken over centre line
Fouls committed — opposing team shoots free shot from centre

3. Net Ball

Same rules as bucketball. Target is basketball hoop.

Score: 1 point if ball hits backboard
                       2 points if ball hits rim of hoop
                       3 points if ball goes in hoop

4. Pillar Ball

Start — toss at centre.
Players run anywhere on the floor.
One post or pillar on each end.
Object — to hit post.
Can't run more than three steps with the ball.
Can't hold the ball for more than 3 seconds.

5. Corner Ball

Equipment: Basketball, the field is an oblong 30' x 40', divided into two equal parts by a centre line. Each part contains two bases three feet square in the four corners.

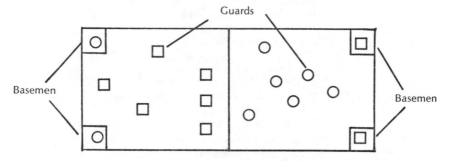

Organization: The group is divided into two teams according to the above diagram. Two members of each team are selected as basemen and occupy the far corners of the opponent's territory. The others are guards. The object of the guards is to pass the ball to the basemen of their team, over the heads of the opposing guards. The object of the guards is to intercept the ball in passing both ways.

Fouls: 1. Carrying the ball (more than one step).
                       2. Striking the ball when it is held by a player.
                       3. Holding, striking or pushing an opponent.
                       4. Stepping out of the field with one or both feet, or over the centre line (guards), or stepping into the bases.
                       5. Stepping out of the bases with one or both feet.

Penalty: The ball is awarded to the guards of the other team.

Scoring: A point is scored when a baseman catches the ball from one of the guards of his own team. It must be a fair throw, i.e., the ball must not touch the ground, wall, or ceiling before being caught by a baseman. If in the course of the play, the ball rolls or is thrown off the field, it must be brought back by a guard of the team whose line it crossed. He must put the ball in play by standing on the line where the ball left the field and throwing it to one of the guards of his own team. Basemen are allowed to jump up and catch the ball, but both feet must land and be kept within the base.

6. Non-Stop Ball

All rules of conventional full-court basketball apply to Non Stop Ball with the following exceptions:

1. Three to eight players may be used on each team.

2. The team scoring at its opponent's basket may continue to score as many times at that basket without any break in the action. In other words, as the ball comes through the net, it is still in play and can be retrieved by either team. If the team that has just scored gets the ball, it may immediately shoot the ball again and score as many times as possible. This is a key feature of the game as it does not allow either team even a very short rest after each basket. Of course, the teacher should be alert for extreme fatigue in any player and remove that player or insert appropriate rest periods for all players when necessary.

3. There are no out-of-bounds. The ball and players may go off the conventional court. The ball may bounce off the side walls but the action does not stop. Only when a hazardous situation arises should the teacher stop play and award the ball to the team nearest the ball.

4. When a foul is called, the ball is immediately handed to the nearest player on the team that had been fouled and the play continues. In the spirit of the game, the rather liberal foul rule should not be abused. If it is abused, the teacher should remove the offending player for an appropriate period. The teacher's main objective is to strive for continuity of action.

FLOOR HOCKEY

Rule 1. Equipment
- plastic equipment - sticks and pucks
- goal - six feet wide and four feet high. (Cosom lists the official size as 72" wide, 54" high, 18" deep)
Goalies crease - 6 foot radius
Penalty shot line - 20 feet from goal

Rule 2. Officials
- referee and penalty keeper

Rule 3. Time of Play
- two periods of ten minutes (at noonhour). Three periods, or longer periods as time permits.

Rule 4. Players
- six players - two forwards, a centre, two guards and a goalie.
- unlimited substitution whenever puck is dead.

Rule 5. Centering the Puck
- the sticks must be in contact with the floor; other players must be outside the centre circle, puck must be swept out of position.

Rule 6. Scoring
- the entire puck must pass beyond the goal posts or across the goal line.
- players may not shoot from within goalie's crease.

Rule 7. Violations
- goal-keeper throwing puck beyond centre.

- puck in crease more than three seconds.
- standing and holding puck against wall.
- catching or holding puck in hands.

PENALTY - face-off

Rule 8. Minor (one minute) Penalties
- goalkeeper going beyond crease.
- offending player in defending team's crease.
- high sticking.
- tripping, roughing, shoving, holding and striking.

Rule 9. Major (two minute) Penalties
- charging from behind.
- deliberate checking into walls.
- throwing a stick at puck or player.
- unsportsmanlike conduct
     (MISCONDUCT - 10 minutes)

Penalty Shots
- defensive player stopping shot in his own crease (other than goalie).
- deliberate fouling of shooter in the clear.

Made or missed, the puck is faced-of at centre.

A player in penalty box can come out when time is up or when the *opposing* team scores a goal. Except a MAJOR penalty.

1. Keep your stick low (below the waist level at all times).
2. Use clean body checks.
3. Play your position.
4. Use team-work.
5. Be on time for all games.
6. Referee's calls are final.

TETHERBALL

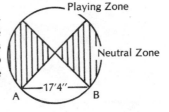

The Court: Lay out a circle 20 feet in diameter. Anywhere on this circle locate two points 17 feet 4 inches apart. From these points, draw two lines through the center of the circle.

No. of Players: 2

Formation: The player who serves first is chosen by lot. The shorter player has choice courts. After the first game the winner serves first. One player stands in each court.

Procedure: The server starts the game by tossing the ball into the air and striking it with his hand or fist in the direction he chooses. His opponent may not strike the ball until it passes him on its second swing around the pole. Server may not strike the ball until his opponent has done so. As the ball travels, each player tries to hit it in an effort to wind the rope completely around the pole. The player who first winds the rope completely around the pole above the foul line and in the direction of his play, wins the game. During the game each player must remain in his own playing zone. The following are fouls:

Fouls:
1. Hitting the ball with any part of the body other than the hands or forearms.
2. Stopping continuous play by holding or catching the ball.
3. Touching the pole with any part of the body.
4. Interfering with the progress of the game by hitting rope with forearm or hands.
5. Playing the ball while standing outside the playing zone.
6. Stepping on the neutral zone lines.
7. Throwing the ball.
8. Winding the ball around the pole below foul mark.
9. Use of two hands together—open or closed.
10. Using pole as an aid in jumping for the ball.
11. Catching rope and throwing rope and ball.

Scoring:
The game is won by the player who first winds the rope completely around the pole above the foul line, or by forfeit because of a foul committed by his opponent. A series consists of two games won out of three. Upon finishing a series, the loser drops out and a new challenger comes into the game. When a player defeats three opponents, he automatically drops out of the game at the conclusion of the third series and two *new* players take the court.

Penalty:
A player who commits any of the fouls listed above forfeits the game to his opponent. Play stops immediately after a foul has been committed.

Teaching Suggestions:
1. Vary the rope lengths on different poles for players of various heights.
2. Provide several courts, balls, and poles. It is recommended that the intermediate and upper-grade level hard surfaced areas *each* have a minimum of four courts.
3. For practice, use a line formation of five or six pupils at a court taking turns hitting the ball without an opponent. Let each pupil have several practice hits before allowing competition.
4. Emphasize keeping the eyes on the ball until contact of the hand is made with the ball — then follow through on the hit. This activity develops hand-eye coordination.
5. Practice foot work for position on the ball so that the hand can hit through the ball.

10-Hit Tetherball

Procedure:

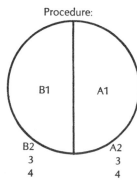

The rules are the same as regular tetherball rules with the following exceptions:
1. This is a team game with the team lined up in single file outside the tetherball area.
2. The game is started in the normal fashion by the first player (B1 and A1) on each team.
3. These first two players have a total of 10 hits to try and score a point.
4. If a point is not scored by one of these players, within the allotted 10 hits, they must retire to the end of the line and the next people A2 and B2 try to further advance the ball toward a score within their 10-hit maximum.

61

5. The rope is not unwound with each new set of players, rather the game is continued where the others left off.
6. The procedure is followed until a team scores a point. Only after a point is scored does the game start over.

Tips:
1. The teacher should stand opposite the tetherball ring from where the teams enter.
2. Until the game is understood the teacher should act as the counter. (Remember each new set of opponents gets a *total* of 10 hits *between* them. Any hits are counted whether the ball is hit alternately by each opponent or consecutively by one).
3. The teacher should count loudly enough so that the players will know when to retire from the area.
4. Children should be encouraged to jump quickly when it's their turn so that the game moves quickly and is continuous.
5. After the game is understood, certain children may be appointed counter.

BATTING GAMES

Lead up to SOFTBALL

1. Danish Rounders

Players: 8 on a team. Teams unlimited.

Equipment: Tennis Ball.

Area: Playground or gymnasium (45-ft. bases)

Skills: Throwing, catching, and base running.

Game: The object is for the batters to touch all bases and score a run without being put out. The pitcher throws the ball slightly above the head of the batter, who tries to hit the ball with his hand. Whether he hits the ball or not, he runs to first base and farther if possible. The fielding team returns the ball to the pitcher who downs the ball on the pitcher's mound. If the ball is downed before the runner reaches a base, he is out. Any number of players may be at a base at the same time, and on a strike or a hit they may or may not choose to run to the next base. When the ball is downed by the pitcher, any base runner off base is out. A caught fly ball puts out not only the batter, but also any players running between bases. Play is continued until all members have batted; then sides change.

Scoring: One point is scored for each run.

Variations: Use a stick bat.

2. Circle Softball

Players: 6 to 8 on a team. Teams unlimited.

Equipment: Softball and bat. (50-ft. circle)

Area: Playground or gymnasium.

Skills: Batting, fielding, pitching, and catching.

Game: The object is for the batting team to hit the ball out of a circle formed by the fielding team. The members of each team are numbered. The pitcher is the member of the fielding team whose number corresponds to that of the batter; thus each batter has a different pitcher. The fielders select a catcher to go into the circle. Each batter tries to hit five strike pitches out of the circle. The leader or umpire calls the strikes. After everyone has batted, sides change.

Scoring: One point is scored for each batted ball that gets outside the circle.

Variations: (1) Use a batting tee.
(2) Adjust the size of the circle to the ability of the players.
(3) Give batter only one try.

3. Cricket Softball

Players: 6 to 8 on a team. Teams unlimited.

Equipment: Softball, 2 bats, 2 Indian clubs, and 2 bases for every two teams.

Area: Playground or gymnasium (bases 25 ft. apart)

Skills: Batting, throwing, catching, and fielding.

Game: The object is for batters to score runs by hitting the ball and running to the opposite base before the Indian clubs can be knocked down by the fielders. There is a batter at each base. Two feet behind each is an Indian club. The fielding team has a pitcher at each base, and the rest of the fielders are scattered around informally. There are no boundaries. The batters assume a position with the thick end of the bat touching the base. One of the pitchers throws the ball underhand at the Indian club from the opposite base. An out is scored every time a pin is knocked down. The batter attempts to protect the pin by hitting the ball. If he hits the ball in any direction, he quickly exchanges places with his teammate on the other base. The fielders try to recover the ball and knock down the pins while the runners are exchanging places. If the fielders do not succeed in knocking down pins in time, a run is scored. The batters may exchange places any number of times on a hit and score a run on every exchange. A player may knock down the pins by throwing the ball at them any time the batter guarding the pins takes his bat off the base. On the pitch, however, the bat on the base is not a protection. A caught fly ball results in an out. Pitchers are rotated after five pitches. The same two batters continue to bat until an out is made. After an out two new batters take over. Three outs retire a side.

Scoring: One point is scored every time the batters exchange places.

Variations: Allow a player only two bats or hits, after which he gives up his place at bat to a teammate. After everyone has batted, teams change sides.

4. Bucket Baseball

Procedure: X-player up to bat picks up three balls and stands in home area to throw the balls quickly (one after the other) in three different directions. He then runs as quickly as possible around the outside of the three bases back to home.
WHILE: fielders chase the balls and must throw each ball from the point of retrieve (no running or moving with a ball in the hands), to the catcher who puts the balls in the basket.

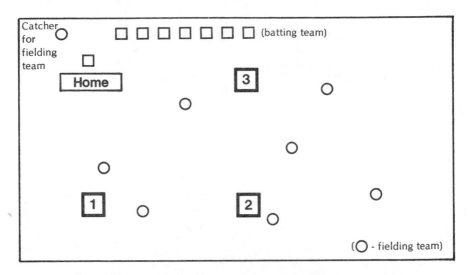

Scoring:	If the X-runner returns *home* before the 0-catcher places the three balls in the basket he scores one point for his team. Each of the X-players has one turn, records the score and changes sides.
Equipment:	1 wastepaper basket 3 small sized Voit rubber utility balls 3 base markers (skittles, bean bags, etc.)
Teams:	From 6-9 per side 2 teams — 1 fielding and 1 batting.

5. Bat Ball

Players:	6 to 8 on a team. Teams unlimited.
Equipment:	Playground ball or volleyball.
Area:	Playground or gymnasium (30 by 50 ft.)
Skills:	Throwing, catching and fielding.
Game:	The object is for the batter to hit the ball into fair territory, circle the far base, and return home without being hit by the ball. The batter bats the ball with his hand or fist so that it crosses the short line; he then attempts to run around the far base and back home without being hit. The members of the fielding team field the ball and attempt to hit the runner with it. The fielders may not walk with the ball or hold the ball longer than three seconds. The runner is not permitted to stop or to run out of the baseline. After everyone bats, sides change.
Scoring:	One point is scored each time a player successfully runs around the far base to home plate without being hit.
Variations.	(1) Use three outs to retire a side. (2) Give the fielders a choice of hitting the runner or throwing to their catcher at home plate ahead of the runner. (3) The fielders must make five passes involving five different players before they may hit the runner.

(4) Have a mat between home and far base where the runner has to perform a stunt going and returning, for example, a forward roll.

6. 2-Pitch Softball

Rules: Same as regulation softball except:

1) Up to 10 players allowed in field at a time.

2) Each team at bat provides its own pitcher. Teams may change pitchers at any time. Pitcher may pitch as soon as his teammate is at bat. (He *does not* wait until defense is set.)

Pitcher throws 2 pitches only per batter. Pitcher must not field, or in any way interfere with a batted ball. If a batted ball inadvertently strikes the pitcher, the ball is still in play.

3) The Batter:

— the batter is allowed 2 pitches only. If he fails to hit a fair ball in 2 pitches, he is *out.*

— bunting is prohibited. The batter is automatically out if he bunts.

— an established batting order must be followed.

4. Base Runners:

— stealing bases is *not* allowed. A base runner may not leave a base until the ball has been hit. A runner leaving before the hit is declared out.

5) When a side is retired (3 outs), play commences as soon as the opposing batter and pitcher are ready for play.

Umpires: a) Home Plate—keeps track of the outs, watches home and third. Makes sure batting order is followed (each team hands in batting order to umpire.)

b) 1st Base—watches 1st and 2nd and for leadoffs. Keeps track of score.

7. Finnish Handball

Area:

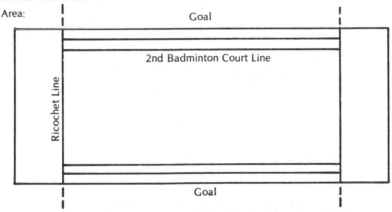

Equipment: One large playball will be placed in the centre of the gym.

Game: Players on each team are numbered off in 3's. When the referee calls a number, all players who are that number are allowed into the centre playing area. They attempt to hit the ball, *with their closed fist only*, so it will touch the wall behind the opposite team, *below shoulder level* and between the two ricochet lines.

The other members of the teams may not come across the second badminton line out from the wall but may stop the ball with their bodies or fists. They are not allowed to use their *feet.*

Penalties: If a person is seen using his feet, crossing the second badminton line or attempting to injure another player, he will be 'kicked out' of the game.

Scoring: One point for each 'goal' scored.

8. Norwegian Ball (Danish Longball)

Players: Any number.

Equipment: One volleyball or one playball.

Area: Suitable for gymnasium, playroom, or playground.

Rules: Team A in field behind centre line of gym. Team B at bat, standing along a given line thus:

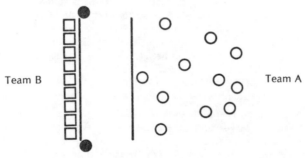

Place an Indian Club or bowling pin at both ends of B's line. The first player on B's team uses volleyball serve to hit ball out into field. The ball must land over center line to be fair. Team A fields the ball and immediately lines up behind player with the ball. The ball is rolled between the legs of all A team to last player. Last player picks up ball and runs to the front of the line holding the ball over the head. In the meantime, the B player who has hit the ball, starts to run around the clubs, counting one run every time the player completes the circuit once. The runner must stop when the ball is held over the head of A player. Continue in this fashion until all B players have had a turn. Add up the number of runs. Now A team goes to bat and B goes to the field.

NOTE: Team may change places after 3 or 4 players have had a turn at bat.

Variations: 1. The B team may throw a playball anywhere in the room which the A team fields and plays in the manner described.
2. Use a baseball diamond. The game is played the same way, but the runner must make a home run to score.

9. Stop

Similar to indoor baseball
Number up to 40 or 50

Rules: Pitcher throws ball in air (underhand) and batter hits ball with fist. Runner attempts to make it safely around the bases to home (1 run). 1 good pitch. May have any number of runners on any one base and runners may pass each other.

Batting team remains up until there are no batters left. When a man is out he goes to a designated area.

Out: Batter out after 1 good pitch.

Batter out if ball caught before it hits the floor (i.e., if caught directly, or on rebound from wall or ceiling).

Runner out if tagged with ball or if ball is returned to pitcher while runner is off base (pitcher calls 'stop').

On a caught ball, runners are out if they are off base or if they have advanced to the next base.

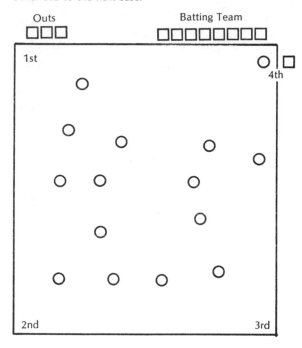

10. V.S.B.

Line up as per diagram. Batter hits ball out of his hand. Fielders must make 4 passes and score basket before runner circles bases. 3 out—side out.

Games

11. Long-Ball

Teams: Two teams, of ten players each.

Ground: A rectangular space, 40 yds. x 20 yds. The longer boundaries to be called the side lines, and the shorter, the goal lines. The main goal line is drawn parallel to the other two and 2 yds. from the top goal line. The space between the top and the main goal lines forms the goal, and the lower boundary is called the back goal line (see plan).

Plan of Field:

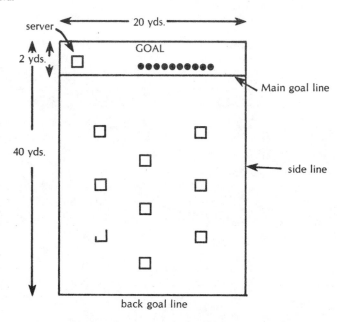

Bat: A "rounders" bat, i.e. a cylindrical bat not more than 20 in. long, not flattened in any way, and measuring not more than 4½ in. round the thickest part.

Ball: A tennis ball (or small lacrosse ball).

Duration of
Play: Forty minutes, with a half-time.

Captains: The captains shall toss for "in" game and decide beforehand on the batting order, on who shall be server, and where the other fielders shall be placed.

"In" game and
"Out" Game: By "in" game is meant batting, by "out" game is meant fielding.

Server: The server only (of the "out" team) shall stand in the goal. He shall warn the batsman before he serves, and must not screw or feint the service. The batsman can claim another service if it is a badly-served ball, provided he has not attempted to hit it. The server is allowed to interrupt the serving by trying to hit an opponent.

The batsmen are allowed three attempts to hit the ball (or one only if this is agreed upon beforehand).

Batsmen:

The "in" game team line up in file facing the server inside the goal. The players hit in succession and in the same order throughout the game. In order to hit the ball again, the player must have scored a run. If a member of the "out" team causes "in" games (see 12 (e) and (f), he gets a reward hit first, otherwise that player starts whose turn it was to hit when last his side got "out". The batsman may hit the ball hard or gently, or not at all; if he misses the ball when properly served, it is counted as a hit. The batsman should aim at hitting the ball beyond the back goal line, and is "out" if one foot is over the line.

The Run:

A run is made when a player, without breaking the rules, has run from goal to back goal line and back again, and the team has had no "out" game in between. The run can be broken by the runner waiting behind the back goal line for a favourable opportunity to complete the run. A batsman need not run on his ball, he can stay in goal, behind the server, and run when an opportunity occurs from another member's hit. Two or more members of the team can be waiting at the top-goal-line or back-goal-line at the same time. The fielders must not actively prevent their opponents from running. No run shall be started while the ball is in the server's hand.

The "out" team gets "in" game if one of the "in" team:
— deliberately touches the ball or hinders the "out" team in fielding.
— hits the ball to ground behind the top-goal-line or the side line (it may roll outside the lines).
— runs over the side line or
— is not in goal to hit.

The "out" team gets "in" game if one of the "out" team:
— hits an "in" team player with the ball when the "in" player has one or both feet in the field or
— catches the ball from a hit.

A ball is caught when a player holds it before it touches the ground. The catcher calls "caught" and drops the ball on the spot where it is caught (unless it is outside the ground, when he must run inside, and place the ball there).

A player is hit if touched by the ball when in the field. He can dodge to avoid the ball provided he does not cross the side lines.

No fielder, except the server, may take more than three steps with the ball in hand. He must aim at a runner or pass to another fielder. If more than three steps are taken with the ball in hand the hit is invalid.

A fielder must not hold the ball more than five seconds. A hit from a ball held longer is invalid.

If there are no runners, the ball must be passed to the server.

If a runner is aimed at by a fielder and missed, he is allowed to run straight back to goal freely or otherwise, and although he may not have reached the back goal-line, he scores a run.

After a hit the bat should be placed on the ground, inside the goal. If it is thrown into the field so that it cannot be reached, it can only be brought back by a player making a run. If this gives "out" game, the new "in" team must bring the bat in themselves.

If a batsman has not run at the end of a round, he must run for a "man's height", i.e. the server throws the ball up about 6 ft. and the batsman must run during that throw.

A runner waiting beyond the back-goal-line must get back to goal before it is his turn to hit again. If he does not, he shall run for a "man's height" throw.

The change from "in" to "out" game shall be made very quickly.

Umpire: The Umpire shall signal to the scorers (two) after each point; call when the players change game, act as timekeeper, and give the result at the end of the game.

That team is the winner which has scored most points.

Bloody Knuckles

Good for
developing:
leg muscles
endurance
peripheral vision and body reaction

Equipment: Benches, balls such as volleyballs or playgrounds balls. Don't use heavy or hard balls.

An arena is made using a wall or walls and the benches. Turn the benches on their side so that the flat side is facing in toward the center.

Rules: The player is out if the ball touches him below the knee. It doesn't matter how it hits him, it is his job to not get hit.

You hit the ball with an open or closed hand (hence the name if you miss it).

You can touch the ball only once unless: the ball rebounds off a player, a wall, or a bench. This means that you cannot dribble the ball, or hold it and then shoot at someone.

If the ball is hit *directly* over the bench the shooter is out. (This is to discourage high shots — injuries). Also, if you use walls you should mark a line, bench-height, in which if the ball is hit directly above this line the shooter would be out.

Variations:
1. SINGLE KNOCKOUT SCRAMBLE
   This game goes on until there is only one player left.
2. SCRAMBLE WITH A TIME LIMIT
   As 1. except there is a time limit of 1, 2, or 3 minutes.
3. TEAM SCRAMBLE WITH A TIME LIMIT
   Two teams playing against each other. The winner is the team who has the most remaining players at the end of time.
4. TEAM GAME NON-STOP SCORE
   Benefit of this — players not out; they return to game.

   As the player is hit, he raises his hand and goes out of the arena to the scorekeeper who records a mark under his team. At the end of a shift (3-5 minutes), the scores are added. The team having the

LEAST marks is the winner.

This variation is the overall most desirable as it keeps all the people in the game.

Cane-Can

Equipment:	2 rubber rings, wicket pins, 2 softball bats, volleyball, playball, or softball
	Small classes can be divided into teams of two or divide the whole class into two teams.
Object of Game:	Everytime the batters exchange places a run is counted. On each hit they may exchange as many times as they like. Therefore the batter stands in front of the wicket with the bat in the ring or hole. The pitcher rolls the ball to the batter who strikes at it. The ball may be hit in any direction and fielders may play anywhere. Batters need not run on a hit unless they feel they can make it between wickets. The batters cannot be put out as long as they have their bats in the ring.
Batters are Out:	—automatically if a fly is caught —if the wickets are knocked down when the bat is out of the hole —if the batter knocks over the wicket.
NOTE:	If playing pairs, one batter out results in the side being out. The next pair up usually are wicket keepers and pitchers who stand just beside the wickets to pitch.

Wickets pins or tin cans

Pitcher ☐   O ←———————————————————→ O   ☐ Pitcher

O Batter   30' - 50'   Batter O

Pundad Ball

A line is drawn to divide length of gym as follows:

(Team #1)

Safety Zone   Fielding Area

Batters

Team #1 at bat. Rest are fielders. Player at bat punches ball into field area and attempts to run to opposite wall and back across dividing line into safety zone without being hit by the ball which may then be thrown at him by any of the fielders.

—a batted ball caught on fly is not out.
—fielders may move only when not in possession of ball
—fielders may pass the ball
—after three outs, switch team

HANDBALL

Handball is played by striking a ball with the hand so that it hits a wall or walls. The front wall is the main playing surface. The ball is hit alternately by opposing players or players on opposing doubles teams. On all points, the ball must hit the front wall, regardless of what other walls it hits, and must be returned by the opponent before it strikes the floor the second time. Points are scored only by the server. The first to score 21 points wins the game. Two, three, or four people can play in singles, three-handed, or doubles competition.

The One-Wall Game

In elementary schools, the one-wall singles game is recommended. The basic rules are:

 1. The server must stand in the serving zone while serving. He must not step over the short line, the service line, or the sideline. (See the diagram).

 2. The server must bounce the ball on the floor within the serving area and hit it on the first bounce.

 3. When served, the ball must first strike the front wall and then bounce over the short line within bounds. On the line is considered in bounds.

 4. A served ball that does not rebound past the short line or lands on the short line is called a short and is not in play.

 5. A served ball landing beyond the back line but inside the side-lines is called a long.

 6. Two successive shorts or a short and a long, or two successive longs constitute a hand-out and loss of service.

 7. If a served ball goes out of bounds, a hand-out results and service reverts to the opponent.

 8. The receiver may not return a long or a short.

 9. In doubles, the server's partner must stand outside the side-lines until the ball is served.

10. Players may strike the ball on the fly or first bounce. A failure to do so — or to comply with the other requirements noted above — results in either loss of service or loss of a point.

11. Interference is called a hinder and results in the point being played over. This also occurs when a player is hit by the ball.

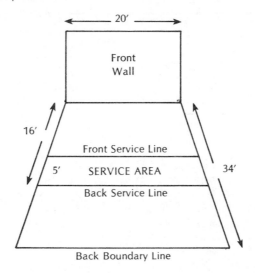

Games

AQUATIC GAMES

Non-Competitive Group Activities

TREADING WATER

Tread water while: holding both hands in the air telling five jokes or a short story catching a ball —(how many times you can catch it out of ten throws) whistle a song or tune.

BALL TAG

People are numbered off and stand in a circle, arms length apart. The instructor throws the ball in the middle of the circle while calling out a number. The person with that number swims toward the ball. Others swim away as fast as they can. The person with their number called yells "stop" as soon as he reaches the ball. The contestant with the ball then tries to hit others with the ball.

COPY CAT

One person is chosen as the leader. He stands in the middle of a circle formed by others. He then performs a stunt that others must do also.

SPAGHETTI

All the players join hands and form a circle. They must not let go of hands! The instructor directs people to weave under and/or over another person's arms. He keeps doing this until they are all linked in one big tangle. The group is given a time limit to get untangled, with letting go of their hands.

CATCH A MAN

The person who is 'it' stands in the middle of the pool and the other players stand at the end of the pool. When the person who is 'it' calls "go", the players try to get to the other end of the pool while swimming and trying to avoid being caught. To be caught, you have to have your head dunked.

BLIND MAN

The group starts at one line and tries to get to the other line 20 meters away. The players have to close their eyes, the teacher calls the strokes for the students to do.

DOGFISH — CATFISH

Name three participants as the catfish, and one as a shark. All of the other participants join hands in a circle and act as a net. The catfish usually start inside the net. The shark tries to tag the catfish. The "net" helps the catfish but hinders the shark by raising and lowering arms, closing the net, etc. If the shark gets in the net, the catfish swim out. The net then tries to keep the shark inside.

VOLTAGE

The students form a circle holding hands in waist deep water. The instructor squeezes the hand of the person beside him. When his hand is squeezed, the pupil submerges his face under water, holds his breath, and passes the squeeze to the next person and so on. When all are submerged, the instructor repeats the same pattern until eveyone is out of the water waist high. (They come up instead of going under the water.)

Games

Team Games
FRUIT COCKTAIL RACE

There are two sides consisting of from four to eight players. The fruit (apples) is placed in the centre of the pool. At the signal, the players dive towards the apples. When he reaches the centre, each player grabs one apple in either hand. Then, he turns and swims back to the starting point using a sidestroke. When he reaches the shore, he places the apples on the dock or side of the pool, turns and again goes for more apples. This continues until there are no apples left in the water. The team retrieving the most apples wins.

Variation: To make this a real fruit cocktail, you can use any type of fruit that floats.

SNATCHBALL

Two teams line up opposite each other. Each player is given a number. The instructor calls out a number and throws the ball to the centre of the swimming area between the two teams. As the number is called out, two players of opposing teams with the same number swim to the ball. The player who gets the ball and reaches home safely with it wins one point for his team. The other player will try to steal the ball. The team with the greatest number of points is declared the winner.

Variations: Call 2 or 3 numbers at a time; To encourage looking under water, use objects that sink and are on the bottom of the pool; If the ball carrier is tagged before returning to his base, then the other team scores a point. Use rubber rings or pucks instead of a ball.

KEEP AWAY

Divide the class into two teams. Give one team a ball. They must keep the ball away from the other team.

UNDER THE LEG

The team forms a line with its players about 3 meters apart. The players stand with their legs apart. The rear man swims under the legs of each member in the line. Players continue until the original order is established. This game may be played in shallow or deep water. Teams should be limited to not more than ten players a side.

OTHER WATER ACTIVITIES
1. Waterpolo.
2. Basic synchronized swimming.
3. Movement to music.

OTHER AQUATIC GAMES

Boat Race

Equipment:	As many innertubes as possible.
Organization:	Split into teams of 3, each team member having an innertube. Teams race from shallow end to deep end and back *as a unit.*. If the team member chain breaks during race, it must be reconnected before proceeding.
Variation:	Teams of 2, 4, 5, or 6 Use paddles or paddleboards.

Water Basketball

Equipment:	Waterpolo ball (playground ball). Baskets may consist of 3 or 4 innertubes tied together and anchored by weight.

Games

Play:	The game is played in the shallow end of swimming pool. The "baskets" float in the pool. The objective, as in regular basketball, is to throw the ball through the hoop.
Rules:	No physical contact (free throw to man fouled). When a player has possession, he may not advance.

Water Volleyball

Equipment:	Waterpolo ball and net.
Play:	Regular volleyball rules are followed (or modifications appearing in this booklet).

Tug-O-War

Equipment:	Strong rope.
Play:	As in regular tug-o-war, teams try to pull centre piece of rope across a pre-designated marker.
Variation:	For better swimmers, both teams in the deep end.

Candle Relay

Equipment:	6" non-drip candles, matches or cigarette lighters.
Organization:	Split into teams. Half of each team at opposite ends of pool.
Play:	Idea is to get lit candle from one end of the pool to the other in relay fashion without extinguishing flame. (Hint: fastest way is on your back or front with candle in your mouth!)
	If flame is extinguished during a leg, team member must return to his/her starting point and re-light candle.

Piggyback Wrestling

Teams of two, with one member on the shoulder of his/her partner (chest deep water). Idea is to try and topple all other pairs.

Water Bucketball

Rules are the same as for bucketball mentioned earlier.

Innertube Waterpolo

1. Maximum of 8 players per team.
2. There are two 15 minute halves, at the end of the first half, the teams switch ends.
3. At the beginning of the games, all the players must be against the end (goal) wall of their wide until the ball is thrown into the center by the referee.
4. No player can dump, grab hold of the tube or body of another player. They may not restrain them or push them away in any manner. If a player is the receiver of any of these fouls, he gains possession of the ball.
5. If a player manages to touch the ball without touching the player who has possession he gets the ball. If the ball is knocked free, then it is a free ball.
6. *Offsides.* An offensive player cannot cross the opponents' line before the ball (e.g. the ball cannot be passed to an offensive player waiting over the line). The ball may be thrown across first or carried across. (Line here means the backstroke flag line at either end of the pool.)
7. If an offside is called, the defending goalie receives the ball.
8. After a goal, the goalie receives the ball and he may not pass it out over the center line.
9. Players must remain in their tubes throughout the play. If, during play, a player upsets his tube, he must get back in it before touching or throwing the ball.

Appendices

Reference Material for Intramurals
A Sample Constitution for an
Intramurals Program
Scheduling Sheet

APPENDIX 1

Reference Material for Intramurals

A. Recommended Texts:
1. *Challenge and Change: A History of NIRSA.* James Clarke, Leisure Press, West Point, N.Y. 1978.
2. *Co-Rec Intramural Sports Handbook.* Manjone and Bowe, Leisure Press, West Point, N.Y. 1978.
3. *Intramural Administration: Theory and Practice.* Peterson (editor), Prentice-Hall, Inc., Englewood Cliffs, N.J. 1975.
4. *Intramural Director's Handbook.* Peterson and Preo (editors), Leisure Press, West Point, N.Y. 1977.
5. *Intramurals: Programming and Administration,* Pat Mueller, 4th ed., Ronald Press Co., New York, 1971.
6. *Intramural Sports: A Text and Study Guide.* H.F. Beeman, C.A. Harding, J.H. Humphrey, Wm. C. Brown Co., Dubuque, Iowa, 1974.
7. *Staging Successful Tournaments,* E.D. Boyden & R.G. Burton, Creative Editorial Service, Hollywood, California, 1973.
8. *Structured Intramurals,* Francis M. Rokosz, W.B. Saunders, Toronto, 1975.
9. *The Organization and Administration of Intramural Sports,* Louis E. Means, C.V.Mosby Co., St. Louis, 1973.

B. Other Texts:
1. *Bibliography of References for Intramurals and Recreational Sports.* McGuire and Mueller, Leisure Press, West Point, N.Y. 1975.

2. *Complete Guide to Administering the Intramural Program.* N.E. Gerou, Parker Publishing Co., West Nyack, N.Y. 1976.
3. *Drug Abuse: Intramurals a Viable Alternative,* P.R. Varnes, S.W. Fagerburg, Kendal Hunt, Dubuque, Iowa.
4. *Intramurals,* Scarborough Board of Education, W.C. Campbell.

C.   Journals and Newsletters:
1. Canadian Intramural Newsletter, Rick Turnbull, Editor, Coord. of Recreation, Athletic Centre, University of Guelph, Guelph, Ontario.
2. NIRSA Newsletter, c/o Will Holsberry (see under Formal Associations).
3. CAHPER Journal, 10th Floor, 333 River Rd., Vanier City, Ont., K1L 8B9
4. JOPER Journal, 1201 Sixteenth St. N.W., Washington, D.C. 20036.
5. NIRSA Journal, P.O. Box 3, West Point, N.Y. 10996

D.   Formal Associations:
1. Canadian Intramural Recreation Association
    Mr. Peter Hopkins, President,
    Department of Athletics,
    University of Waterloo,
    Waterloo, Ontario.
2. National Intramural-Recreational Sports Association (NIRSA)
    Dr. Will Holsberry, Executive Secretary,
    Dixon Rec. Centre, Oregon State University,
    Corvallis, Oregon 97331
3. National Intramural Sports Council (NISC) — affiliate of AAHPER
    American Alliance for Health, Physical Education, and Recreation
    c/o NISC Publicity Coordinator,
    1201 16th Street, N.W.
    Washington, D.C. 20036
    (202) 833-5541

APPENDIX 2
A Sample Constitution for an Intramurals Program

ARTICLE I — NAME

This organization will be known as Intramural Sports.

ARTICLE II — OBJECTIVES

To promote and provide all students with opportunities for:

1. Physical and mental health and fitness
2. Personal and group enjoyment
3. Recreation, present and future
4. Socio-psychological development

ARTICLE III — ELIGIBILITY

Section 1. All students are eligible to enter any intramural activity except as provided by the following rules.

Section 2. Any student currently competing as a school representative in any sport may not participate in the said sport in intramural activity. Special consideration may be obtained from the Selection Committee. Also, eligibility rules may vary according to individual sports and participants are referred to those rules.

Section 3. A person can participate for only one team per sport during the year. The team he/she first represents will be the only team for which he/she can play in that sport for the remainder of the year, unless otherwise directed by the Selection Committee.

Section 4. Each team will be required to submit an official entry sheet listing all participating members by the date specified by the Selection Committee.

    a) a player not on the roster sheet for that activity will be considered an ineligible player.
    b) eligible players may be added to the team roster via the Selection Committee, but this must be done at least 24 hours prior to the competition in which the new players will play. After the third week of competition (if applicable), only teams in the lower half of the standings will be allowed to add players.
    c) Players signing up on an individual basis to play team sports will be assigned to a team (new or existing) by the Selection Committee.

Section 5. Teams contravening any of the above eligibility rules will forfeit all games in which they were involved.

Section 6. All rules for each intramural sport will be published and made available to each team. It is the responsibility of every team captain or manager to ensure that individual team members known the rules.

ARTICLE IV — PROTESTS

Section 1. A team captain or manager may protest:

    a) on the playing of ineligible player(s); or
    b) when an interpretation of the rules is in doubt and actually involves the score. A protest can be made in this case *only* when no referee is present

Section 2.

    a) All protests must be made on the official protest form to the Activities and Rules Committee within 24 hours of the contest in question.
    b) Where necessary, both contestants and the officials in charge will be permitted to present their version of the case before a decision is made.

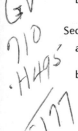

Appendices

c) No protest may be entered on any judgment of an official.
d) All protests involving eligibility must be noted to the referee (to the other team captain in the event of no referee) prior to the start of a contest, or upon entry of a suspected ineligible player. The referee informs both team captains that the game is being played under protest. This protest can be withdrawn if the alleged ineligible player(s) does not play in the game.
e) After investigating a protest, a decision will be made by the Activities and Rules Committee. This decision may be appealed to the Intramurals Council, whose decision is final.

ARTICLE V — FORFEITS, POSTPONEMENTS, CANCELLATIONS

Section 1. A forfeit will occur when, according to the rules for that sport, a team has too few players to start the game.

a) a team will be allowed 5 minutes after the officially scheduled starting time for a contest before a forfeit is declared unless otherwise specified by rules for that particular sport.
b) the official or supervisor in charge of the contest will declare the forfeit.
c) if a team leaves before the forfeit is duly noted by an official or supervisor, then both teams will be credited with a forfeit.
d) the team that is present at a forfeit must have the minimal complement of players allowed for that sport or both teams will be given a forfeit.
e) two consecutive forfeits by a team will result in that team being eliminated from the sport for that year at the discretion of the Activities and Rules Committee.

Section 2. In case of inclement weather, it is the responsibility of team captains to find out if the game has been postponed or cancelled by checking the intramurals notice board. If notice of postponement or cancellation is not given, teams must show up for the game.

ARTICLE VI — CONDUCT OF PARTICIPANTS

While most competitors observe the spirit of intramurals, the following guidelines are necessary:

Section 1. Conduct — Any incidents involving fighting, striking an official, deliberate injury or attempts to injure, swearing or profane language, will be dealt with severely.

Section 2. Sportsmanship — Individual players and teams are expected to act in a sportsmanlike manner at all times during intramural competition. Sportsmanship embraces any incident or action, on or off the field of play, which the Intramurals Council feels is detrimental to the proper functioning of an activity and to the best interests of other players. Any incident(s) of unsportsmanlike conduct will be handled by the Intramurals Council with a player(s) or team subject to suspension.

ARTICLE VII — POINTS SYSTEM

Three points shall be given for each victory, two points for each tie, one point for each loss, and no points for a forfeit.

ARTICLE VIII — SAFETY

Section 1. Accident prevention and safety should be a prime concern for organizers, officials and participants. All safety policies and procedures should be strictly adhered to.

Section 2. All injuries sustained in intramural play must be reported immediately to the staff advisor or supervisor on duty.

Section 3. Injuries should be handled promptly by the supervisor on duty.

ARTICLE IX — AMENDMENTS

By-laws may be amended at any time by majority vote of the Intramurals Council.

APPENDIX 3
Scheduling Sheet

This sheet can be used as a quick reference for scheduling games in a Round Robin League or Tournament for 4 to 10 teams.

Note: 1. Games involving *even* numbers of teams are scheduled by holding team #1 stationary and rotating clockwise all other teams, one step at a time.

2. Games involving *odd* numbers of teams are scheduled by holding X stationary and rotating clockwise all teams, one step at a time. The team opposite X then receives a bye for that week.

4 Teams

1	2	1	4	1	3
4	3	3	2	2	4

5 Teams

1	2	5	1	4	5	3	4	2	3
5	3	4	2	3	1	2	5	1	4
X	4	X	3	X	2	X	1	X	5

6 Teams

1	2	1	6	1	5	1	4	1	3
6	3	5	2	4	6	3	5	2	4
5	4	4	3	3	2	2	6	6	5

7 Teams

1	2	7	1	6	7	5	6	4	5	3	4	2	3
7	3	6	2	5	1	4	7	3	6	2	5	1	4
6	4	5	3	4	2	3	1	2	7	1	6	7	5
X	5	X	4	X	3	X	2	X	1	X	7	X	6

8 Teams

1	2	1	8	1	7	1	6	1	5	1	4	1	3
8	3	7	2	6	8	5	7	4	6	3	5	2	4
7	4	6	3	5	2	4	8	3	7	2	6	8	5
6	5	5	4	4	3	3	2	2	8	8	7	7	6

9 Teams

1	2	9	1	8	9	7	8	6	7	5	6	4	5	3	4	2	3
9	3	8	2	7	1	6	9	5	8	4	7	3	6	2	5	1	4
8	4	7	3	6	2	5	1	4	9	3	8	2	7	1	6	9	5
7	5	6	4	5	3	4	2	3	1	2	9	1	8	9	7	8	6
X	6	X	5	X	4	X	3	X	2	X	1	X	9	X	8	X	7

10 Teams

1	2	1	10	1	9	1	8	1	7	1	6	1	5	1	4	1	3
10	3	9	2	8	10	7	9	6	8	5	7	4	6	3	5	2	4
9	4	8	3	7	2	6	10	5	9	4	8	3	7	2	6	10	5
8	5	7	4	6	3	5	2	4	10	3	9	2	8	10	7	9	6
7	6	6	5	5	4	4	3	3	2	2	10	10	9	9	8	8	7